European Steam

in the 1960s

BRITISH RAILWAYS

PASSENGER SERVICES

LONDON
(Paddington)

BRISTOL & WEST OF ENGLAND

SOUTH & NORTH WALES

BIRMINGHAM, GLOUCESTER, WORCESTER,
WEST MIDLANDS
(including Suburban Services)

11th SEPTEMBER 1961
to 17th JUNE 1962
(or until further notice)

Supplements, giving details of alterations to this timetable,
are issued free of charge, see page 2.

ONE SHILLING

Situated in south-east Hungary, Békéscsaba is a significant railway junction with connections through to Budapest, Szeged and across the border to Bucharest and Arad in Romania. On 3 September 1964 two 2-6-2Ts operated by Magyar Államvasutak (MÁV; Hungarian State Railways) are seen. On the left is No 375.598 whilst on the right – and seemingly out of use – is No 376.617. MÁV first introduced the Class 375 in 1907 in response to the number of new branch lines then being opened and the increasing age of the locomotives allocated to branch-line work. For such work, the axle limit was 10.3 tonnes; the early Class 375 just achieved this but later examples were heavier whilst the smaller Class 376, which was first introduced in 1910, was lighter. Production of both types continued for some years; indeed the last steam locomotive constructed for MÁV – in 1959 – was an example of Class 375.
Les Folkard/Online Transport Archive

European Steam
in the 1960s

Peter Waller

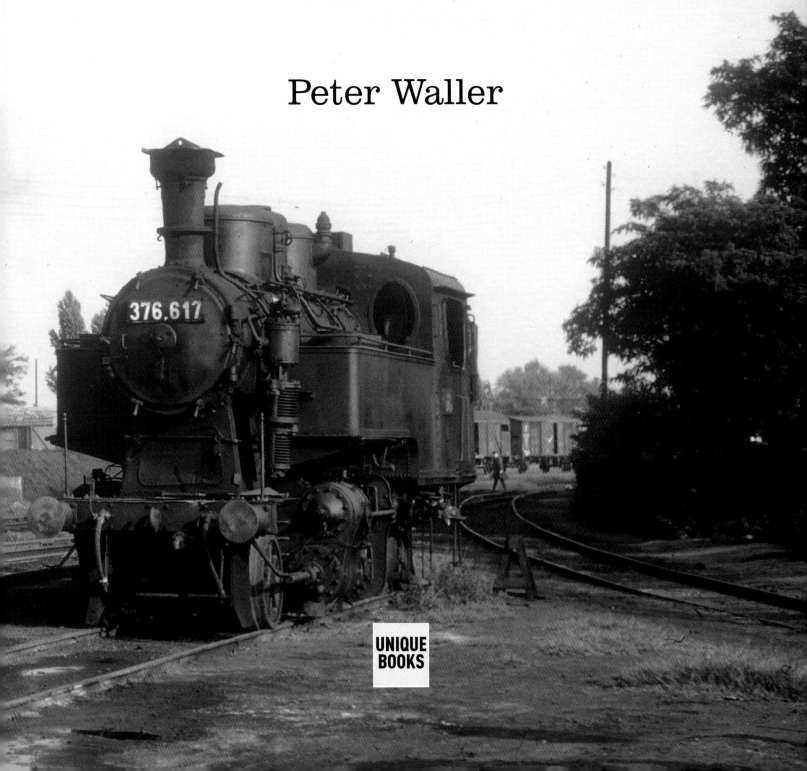

UNIQUE
BOOKS

A note on the photographs and images
All of the photographs in this book have been drawn from the collection of the Online Transport Archive, a UK-registered charity that was set up to accommodate collections put together by transport enthusiasts who wished to see their precious images secured for the long-term. Tickets are from the author's collection whilst the timetables are from the author's collection and that of the Bus Archive. Further information about the archive can be found at: www.onlinetransportarchive.org or email secretary@onlinetransportarchive.org

First published in the United Kingdom
by Unique Books 2020

© Text: Peter Waller 2020

© Photographs: As credited

ISBN: 978 0 9957493 8 2

A CIP record for this book is available from the British Library

Unique Books is an imprint of Unique Publishing Services Ltd,
3 Merton Court, The Strand, Brighton Marina Village, Brighton BN2 5XY.

www.uniquebooks.pub

Printed in Poland

Contents

Introduction

At the end of World War 2 steam traction was still the primary motive power in most European countries. There were exceptions – such as Switzerland – where the pre-war years had seen a considerable investment in electrification, but for most countries diesel and electric traction remained secondary. A generation later, at the end of the 1960s, steam traction was on the retreat in most Western European countries; indeed had been eliminated from the railways of a number of countries, such as Great Britain and the Republic of Ireland. In Eastern Europe, however, steam was to remain dominant for at least a further decade.

There were a number of factors that resulted in the decline of steam traction in the west. Diesel and electric locomotives were more efficient in labour terms and were cleaner operationally. They were more efficient and thus, at a time when the economics of railway operation were deteriorating, offered savings that might ensure great viability. This was certainly the case in Britain, where the introduction of diesel multiple-units following the Modernisation Plan on 1955 saw improvements in the finances of a number of marginal routes; in the event, these were not sufficient to see many of the lines saved in the 1960s. As the railway network of Britain declined in the 1960s, so too did those of many other countries and the reduction in route mileage was a further factor in the decline of steam: quite simply, as the networks declined so too did the requirement for motive power. Another factor was the gradual loss of freight traffic from the railways to an increasingly dominant road network.

In Eastern Europe, however, other factors were at play. Coal in its various forms was widely available whilst supplies of oil were much more limited. The planned economies of the communist governments of the Warsaw Pact could ill-afford the foreign currency required to purchase significant quantities of oil with the result that steam continued to provide the primary motive power. Moreover, many of the lines that, in the west, might have been consigned to the history books were to survive longer as private cars and commercial vehicles were much less prevalent.

In a number of countries, such as Finland, Italy and Sweden, whilst steam may have officially ceased, significant numbers of steam locomotives were retained as part of a 'strategic reserve' in case of problems in the supply of oil or electricity. This meant that, when the reserve was finally disbanded, there were a significant number of steam locomotives that became available for preservation.

This book is a portrait of steam operation primarily during the 1960s; it was a decade of major changes in most countries of Europe – but particularly in the west where many of the traditional mores that had underpinned society for generations increasingly came under attack. For railway photographers it was the first decade in which colour film was more widely available and many of the then relatively young enthusiasts took advantage both of the increased opportunity to travel – a consequence of rising living standards and more disposable income – and of colour film to record the changing railway scene.

Some five decades on, the scenes that these photographers recorded have long vanished. Most of the steam locomotives photographed have been consigned to the scrapyard whilst many of the lines featured are also now but memories. Within some 200 images it is impossible to provide comprehensive overage of each individual nation's operational steam locomotives during the period; it is hoped that this snapshot will provide a potent reminder of what there was and what has been lost. Examples of many of the classes featured are still extant, although for many of those examples still 'dumped' in Eastern Europe and the Balkans the future is not necessarily rosy. Preservation can help to remind people of the past, but it can never replace the reality; all the images in the book record steam at work. There may be the occasional special – inevitable, for example, when recording steam operation in Switzerland – but these are very much in the minority.

Looking back from the cusp of the third decade of the 21st century, we can be but grateful for the amount of time, money and effort that these photographers expended in recording a rapidly changing continent.

Above: In the early years of the 20th century Danske Statsbaner (DSB; Danish State Railways) undertook the replacement of a number of older locomotives. Amongst the new classes that emerged at the time was the Class D (I) 2-6-0, of which 41 were built between 1902 and 1907 primarily for freight traffic. Initially allocated to Jutland, later examples were based on Funen and Zealand. In 1925 work started on rebuilding the class; although the majority were rebuilt by the end of the decade it was not until 1940 that the last was completed. No 838, illustrated here, was originally built by Nydqvist & Holm AB (later NOHAB) of Trollhättan in Sweden during 1907 and was to undergo rebuilding in 1928. Involved in an accident at Nørager in 1956, No 838 was finally to be withdrawn in 1964. Three of the type – Nos 802/25/26 – survive in preservation. *Geoffrey Morant/Online Transport Archive*

Opposite above: DSB Class Q 0-8-0T No 350 is recorded at Fredericia, its home depot, during the summer of 1965. The 15-strong 'Q' class was the last steam locomotive design produced for DSB and the only type not to be based on overseas drawings. Built by Frichs of Aarhus, the first of the type emerged in 1930 with the last – No 350 – emerging in 1945. The locomotives were designed for shunting purposes in marshalling yards. No 350 is now preserved on the Geesthachter Railway in Germany, having been acquired in 1981, whilst sister locomotive No 345 is preserved at the Danish National Railway Museum in Odense. *Harry Luff/Online Transport Archive*

Opposite below: Between 1878 and 1902 DSB took delivery of 45 0-4-0Ts from a number of manufacturers for use as shunting locomotives. Designated Class Hs, the first seven – Nos 378-84 – were supplied by the Glasgow-based Neilson, Reid & Co. Of the seven Scottish-built locomotives, two were withdrawn during the 1930s and one in the 1950s; No 378, which was based latterly at Slagelse, was stored from 1961 until withdrawal in 1964. It is pictured here shortly after withdrawal. *Harry Luff/Online Transport Archive*

Above: Apart from the main DSB network, Denmark also possessed a significant number of private railways such as the Østsjællandske Jernbane Selskab (ØSJS; East Zealand Railway) that operates from Køge, to the south of Copenhagen via Hårlev to Faxe Ladeplads and Rødvig. In1950 the railway purchased two Henschel und Sohn 2-6-0s second-hand from the Kolding Sydbaner (KS: Kolding Southern Railway); No 5 – seen here in August 1966 – was originally built in 1912 whilst sister No 7 was manufactured the previous year. No 5 was withdrawn during 1966 and sold later the same year but was to be scrapped in 1973. No 7, however, was preserved. The railway – now known as Østbanen (the East Railway) – remains operational.

Phil Tatt/Online Transport Archive

Left: Between 1924 and 1928 Borsig-Werke, of Tegel near Berlin, and the Aarhus-based Frichs Maskinfabrik og Kedelsmedie supplied 20 Class S three-cylinder 2-6-4Ts for use on the suburban services into Copenhagen. The first two – Nos 721 and 722 – were built by Borsig-Werke with the Danish company supplying the remainder. With the progressive electrification of the services for which they were designed, the type was withdrawn from service from the early 1960s and No 737 – seen here at Helsingør– was withdrawn in 1969 and scrapped the following year. Three of the class – Nos 736, 739 and 740 – are preserved in Denmark; the last of these spent some years based on the Nene Valley Railway and appeared in the James Bond film *Octopussy*, which was partially filmed on the preserved line.
Paul de Beer/Online Transport Archive

Above: The 'C' class 4-4-0s were introduced in 1903 and were the first inside cylinder locomotives delivered to DSB since 1847. Five – Nos 701-05 – were initially delivered; these were built by Maschinenfabrik Esslingen and were followed in 1909 by a further 15 – Nos 706-20 – that were constructed by another German manufacturer, Berliner Maschinenbau AG (BMAG). The locomotives were allocated to services in Zealand throughout their operational career and, in August 1966, one of the BMAG-built examples – No 710 – is seen awaiting its next duty at Dybbølsbro shed in Copenhagen. Withdrawal of the type commenced in the mid-1950s. Having appeared in the film *Komtessen* in 1961, No 710 was to be the last of the class to be withdrawn – in 1969 – and was scrapped in 1970. One of the class – No 708 – survives in preservation.
Phil Tatt/Online Transport Archive

Above: Between 1914 and 1916 a total of 11 'F' class 4-6-2s were constructed for Swedish Railways by Nydquist & Holm (NOHAB) but, following main-line electrification, the entire class was sold to DSB. Impressed by the performance of the type, DSB ordered a further 25 in 1942; these were built by the Aarhus-based builder Frichs between 1942 and 1950. The ex-Swedish locomotives were numbered 964-74 whilst the 1942 batch became Nos 975-99. The last of the batch – No 999 – is seen here at Naestved on 1 September 1967. Preserved on withdrawal in 1976, No 999 was to be severely damaged by fire in November 1981 and subsequently scrapped. Two of the ex-Swedish locomotives – Nos 964 and 966 – have been preserved in Sweden whilst a further four – including No 996 based at Railworld on the Nene Valley Railway – of the Frichs-built examples also survive.
John Worley/Online Transport Archive

Above: On 17 May 1960 Valtionrautatiet (VR; Finnish Railways) Class Vr1 (originally Class L1) 0-6-0T No 791 is pictured shunting at Hyvinkää. A total of 43 of this powerful type of locomotive were built between 1913 and 1927 by Oy Tampella Ab and Hanomag (Hannoversche Maschinenbau AG) with the last surviving in service until 1974. Like a number of countries, Finland retained a significant number of steam locomotives as part of a strategic reserve in case of war rendering the electrified network inoperable or diesel supplies being restricted. As a result a significant number of the 'Vr1' class have survived in preservation – some 18 in all – in Finland and elsewhere; No 791 is, however, not one of the survivors.

Charles Firminger/Bob Bridger Collection/Online Transport Archive

Opposite above: Pictured at Riihimäki with the 12 noon service from Haapamäki to Helsinki is VR Class Hr1 (originally Class P1) 4-6-2 No 1011. A total of 22 of the class were constructed by Oy Lokomo Ab and Oy Tampella Ab between 1937 and 1957; the type was nicknamed 'Ukko-Pekka' ('Grandpa Pekka') after Pehr Evind Svinhufvud who was president of Finland between 1931 and 1937. Although all were taken out of service by the end of 1971, two were temporarily restored to service in 1974 as a result of the oil crisis. A number of the class – including No 1011 at Otanmäki – survive in preservation.
Charles Firminger/Bob Bridger Collection/Online Transport Archive

Opposite below: Two VR 2-8-2Ts – Nos 763 and 772 – and a 2-8-2 – No 1047 – are seen outside Helsinki (Pasila) shed on 21 May 1962. These were built to operate on the VR standard 5ft 0in gauge. Concerned by the low speed and power of their existing motive power on suburban services into Helsinki, VR ordered a batch of six 2-8-2T locomotives – Nos 761-66 – from the German manufacturer Hanomag; delivered in 1924, these locomotives were initially designated Class N1 and were latterly Class Pr1. A further 10 – Nos 767-76 – were built under licence in Finland by Oy

Lokomo Ab and Oy Tampella Ab with the last being delivered in 1926. Generally the locomotives operated with smokeboxes pointing in the Helsinki direction. No 1047 was one of the 67 locomotives constructed between 1940 and 1957 that comprised the Class Tr1 (originally Class R1) that were built by the Oy Lokomo Ab and Oy Tampella Ab companies as well as the German-based Arnold Jung Lokomotivfabrik. The last of the class – No 1096 – was the last steam locomotive to be constructed for VR. The last of the type were withdrawn in 1975 and some 20 survive in preservation, including two – Nos 1060 and 1077 – in Britain.
Les Folkard/Online Transport Archive

Above: On 21 May 1962 one of the German-built examples – No 764 – of Class Pr1 is seen heading through Pasila – to the north of central Helsinki and location of major railway yards – with a service towards the north-east. Use of the type on suburban services declined during the 1960s as electric services took over and the locomotives were used thereafter on freight traffic. All were withdrawn by the end of 1972 although one – No 776 – survives in preservation.
Les Folkard/Online Transport Archive

Right: During the first decade of the 20th century VR acquired three types of 2-6-4T; the first were supplied were supplied the US-based Baldwin Locomotive Works, with the remaining two classes being built the by the Finnish manufacturer Tampella. No 488 – seen here at Mikkeli (a town more than 200km to the north-east of Helsinki) on 24 May 1962 – was one of seven members of the Class I3 (later Class Vk3) built between 1906 and 1909. The type was capable of being fired by either coal or – as with this example – wood. The last of the type was withdrawn in 1964 with one example – No 489 – now preserved.
Les Folkard/Online Transport Archive

Right: Wood-burning 2-8-0 No 852 is pictured on shed at Pieksämäki on 24 May 1962 having just been refuelled. Nicknamed 'The Little Jumbo', the 'Tk3' class was designed for freight traffic, with the first 100 – Nos 800-99 – being built between 1927 and 1930 and a further 61 being completed between 1943 and 1953. As such, the type was the most numerous class of steam locomotive built for operation in Finland. With a light axle loading, the locomotives were ideal for operation on secondary routes although they were also to be found at the head of stopping services on main lines. All withdrawn by the end of 1975, more than half of the later batch of the type survive in preservation although only two of the original 100 – including No 852 still based at Pieksämäki – are still extant.
Les Folkard/Online Transport Archive

Left: Recorded passing at Pitkälahti on 25 May 1962 are Class Hv3 4-6-0 No 643 and Class Tv1 2-8-0 No 907; the latter is fitted with a spark arresting chimney indicating that it is wood fired. The former was one of 24 locomotives originally introduced as Class H9 in 1921 for express passenger duties. The locomotives were built by a number of contractors; No 643 was one of those constructed by Berlin-based L. Schwartzkopff in 1921. The final examples of the type were withdrawn in 1970; three – Nos 781, 995 and 998 – survive in preservation. Nicknamed 'Jumbo', the first of the 'Tv1' class was introduced in 1917 with 142 being completed between then and 1945, making it the second most numerous class of steam locomotive on VR. Designated as Class K3 prior to 1942, the locomotives were built by five different manufacturers and the last were withdrawn from service in the mid-1970s. Four survive in preservation.
Les Folkard/Online Transport Archive

Above: The Class Hv4 4-6-0 was first introduced in 1912 with a total of 28 being constructed by Oy Lokomo Ab and Oy Tampella Ab. Finnish locomotive class designation were based upon type of traffic and axle loading, so that with this class was 'H' for a passenger tender locomotive with the 'v' indicating axle loading (in this case 11 to 14 tonnes) and the '4' indicating the fourth type 'Hv'. This particular example – No 745 seen at Tampere on 26 May 1962 – was fitted for burning wood. The large spark-arresting chimney contained blades that were arranged that a vortex was induced in the exhaust, resulting in any sparks being extinguished before they could escape the chimney. All of the type were withdrawn by the end of 1964 with Nos 742 and 751 being preserved.
Les Folkard/Online Transport Archive

Left: Between 1901 and 1922 Norsk Stats Jernbane (NSB; Norwegian State Railways) acquired 42 0-6-0Ts of Classes 25a, 25b, 25c, 25d and 25e. The first were constructed by SLM in Switzerland and therefore owed much to the design of the Swiss Class E3/3 primarily for shunting purposes. Three of the type Nos 422 – seen here in May 1961 – 424 and 425 were rebuilt for use on the Flåmsbana (Flåm Railway) whilst five others were sold to SBB in 1947. One of the type – No 227 – is preserved. The 12½-mile Flåmsbana, which links Myrdal with Flåm, was opened in 1940 with electric traction being introduced three years later.
LRTA (London Area) Collection/Online Transport Archive

Right: In July 1962 NSB Class 18c 4-6-0 No 158 is seen at Neleug station. Originally introduced as Class 18a in 1900, 10 of the type – Nos 131-38/57/58 – were constructed between then and 1907 primarily for use on Nordbanen (Northern Railway) Division covering the lines between Grefsen-Røykenvik, Grefsen-Gjøvik and Reinsvoll-Skreia. All, with the exception of Nos 135 and 157, were subsequently modified to become part of Class 18c. No 158 was one of two constructed at the Hamar Iron Foundry in 1903. When withdrawn in 1968, sister locomotive No 134 was the oldest operational steam locomotive with NSB. None of the original Class 18a locomotives survive although one of the later original Class 18c type – No 255 – is preserved.
Phil Tatt/Online Transport Archive

Above: On 20 May 1962 two of the 2-4-4Ts operated by the Trafikaktiebolaget Grängesberg-Oxelösund Järnväger (TGOJ; Grängesberg-Oxelösund Railways) – Nos 91 and 56 – are pictured at Eskilstuna, to the north of Nyköping. The railway, which was only to become part of the national network in the late 1980s following a reconstruction of the Swedish steel industry in the late 1970s, was first established in 1896 but incorporated a number of earlier lines. The railway's core business was the movement of iron ore from Bergslagen to the ironworks at Oxelösund. The railway operated a number of the relatively rare 2-4-4T type; the two illustrated were both built by Motala Verkstad. No 56 was new in 1930 and was initially built for the Oxelösund-Flen-Västermanlands Järnväg (OFWJ; Oxelösund, Flen, Västermanlands Railway) and passed to the TGOJ the following year; it was eventually scrapped in 1964. No 91 was older, being new in 1923 when it entered service with the Landskrona-Lund-Trälleborg Järnväg (LLTJ; Landskrona, Lund, Trelleborg Railway); it

passed to the TGOJ in 1938 and, on withdrawal in 1963, was to be preserved. It is the sole example of the 2-4-4Ts operated by the TGOJ to survive.
Les Folkard/Online Transport Archive

Above: In order to haul the iron ore traffic over the Kiruna to Riksgränsen line, Statens Järnvägar (SJ; Swedish State Railways) constructed the Class Ma 2-8-0; in addition the similar Class Mb was built for traffic on the Gällivare to Luleå. Initially 20 Class Ma were constructed between 1902 and 1907 with a 21st being added following the rebuilding of Class Mb No 651. However, following the electrification of the Kiruna to Riksgränsen line in 1922, the entire class – with three exceptions – were withdrawn and scrapped in the mid-1920s. Two – Nos 657 and 917 – were rebuilt and redesignated as Class Md; these were both scrapped in the late 1930s. The only survivor was No 779, which was originally built by NOHAB in 1904, that was preserved at the railway museum at Tomteboda, where it is seen on 28 May 1962.
Les Folkard/Online Transport Archive

Opposite above: Constructed between 1909 and 1919 a total of 96 Class B 4-6-0s were supplied to SJ by either Motala Verkstad or Nydqvist & Holm AB (NOHAB). Designed for either passenger or freight traffic, the type was to prove successful. In the 1930s, 11 of the type were sold to private operators, although 10 of these were to return to SJ ownership following the nationalisation of the railways. Four were acquired by the Stockholm-Västerå-Bergslagens Järnväg (SWB) during 1936 and 1937 and this company commissioned the construction of a further three from NOHAB during 1943 and 1944. This trio were eventually to become SJ Nos 1695-97 and one of these – No 1696 – is pictured at Rättvik, in the Dalarna province (where the trio was allocated for freight traffic during the 1960s), on 30 May 1962. A number of the Class B type were retained by SJ following the cessation of regular steam operation as part of the country's strategic reserve and were not finally disposed of until after 1990. It was not until 2016 that Sweden finally eliminated its final strategic reserve. As a result of their longevity, s significant number of 'B' class locomotives – including No 1696 as part of the Swedish Railway Museum – survive.
Les Folkard/Online Transport Archive

Below: Following on from the earlier 2-8-0s designed to cater for the iron ore traffic from Kiruna, SJ acquired five powerful Class R 0-10-0s during 1908 and 1909. The first two – Nos 974 and 975 – were constructed by AB Motala Verkstad whilst the remaining three – Nos 976-78 – were completed by NOHAB. These were the most powerful steam locomotives acquired by SJ but further examples of the type were not bought as electrification of the line rendered them redundant. With the type transferred to the Norra Stambanan (Northern Main Line), the two Motala-built examples were sold in 1935 to the Gävle-Dala Järnväg (Gävle to Dala Railway); one of these was scrapped in 1948 but the other – No 975 was returned to SJ in 1948. When recorded here No 977 – seen at Korsnäs on the Finnish-Swedish border on 30 May 1962 – the surviving members of the class were largely employed on lime traffic between Falun and Rättvik. No 975 was exchanged for DSB 964 (ex-SJ Class F 4-6-2 No 1200), which was preserved. Nos 977 and 978 were both scrapped in 1973 with No 976 being preserved. *Les Folkard/Online Transport Archive*

Right: Two SJ locomotives – 2-6-2T No 1614 and 0-8-0T No 1245 – are seen in Malmö on 1 June 1962. In 1941 – with the Nationalisation of the Malmö-Ystads Järnväg (Malmö-Ystad Railway) and Ystad-Eslövs Järnväg (YEJ; Ystad-Eslövs Railway), SJ acquired six powerful 2-6-2Ts; these became Class S6 Nos 1614-19. The type – supplemented by the similar Class S4 (reclassified as Class S6 in 1947) Nos 1610-13 (acquired following the Nationalisation of the Boräs-Alvesta Järnväg in 1940) – continued to operate on the branches of southern Sweden until the lines closed in the 1950s.

Retained as part of the strategic reserve, all bar two – Nos 1611 and 1617 – were scrapped in the early 1970s. No 1614 was originally YEJ No 3 and was built by Motola in 1912. No 1245 was one of 44 Class Na locomotives modified from the earlier Class N 0-8-0Ts. The type had originally been introduced in 1900 for banking and shunting duties, but their usefulness had resulted in further examples being constructed between 1912 and 1920. By this date, a total of 64 had been completed; however, 44 were modified with a superheater between 1922 and 1932, being redesignated as Class Na (or Class N from 1942). Used widely in yards and docks, the majority of the type were scrapped in the early 1970s although Nos 576, 641 and 1169 survive in preservation. No 1245 was built by the Stockholm-based Aktiebolaget Atlas in 1915 and rebuilt a decade later. It was withdrawn and scrapped in 1973.
Les Folkard/Online Transport Archive

Above: The 891mm-gauge Byvalla-Långshyttans Järnväg, which extended about 17½ miles, was constructed to serve the Rällingsberg iron quarrying area in and around Långshyttan. The first section of the line opened for freight traffic on 1 May 1891 with passenger traffic – normally carried in mixed trains – being introduced on 3 May 1893. The bulk of the line closed on 13 November 1964 and was dismantled between 1965 and 1967; the final section, which served the blast furnace at Klosterverken in Långshyttan survived until 11 November 1971. The line employed 10 locomotives all of which were tank engines with the exception of No 5 *Thor* which was an 2-8-0. Here No 5 is seen arriving at Långshyttan station, a building that is still extant, in 1963. The locomotive was built by Falun in 1909 and remained in service until the line's closure; displayed in front of the closed station for a number of years, it was sold in 1974 to the Uppsala-Lanna museum line.
Charles Firminger/Bob Bridger Collection/Online Transport Archive

Above: The Isle of Wight possessed a small railway network physically separated from the rest of the system, although there had been plans – never completed – to link the two via a tunnel under the Solent. Although much of the network had closed by the start of the 1960s, two sections – from Cowes to Ryde via Newport to Ryde and Ryde to Ventnor – survived and here one of the 0-4-4Ts – No W33 *Bembridge* – passes over the River Medina in Newport as it heads east towards Ryde with a train from Cowes. Both sections of route were listed for closure in the Beeching report – *The Reshaping of British Railways* – in March 1963 but the Ryde to Shanklin section of the route to Ventnor was reprieved and electrified using redundant London Underground tube stock; this was necessary as the loading gauge on the island was restricted and British Railways lacked suitable rolling stock for the new service. Services from Cowes to Ryde were withdrawn on 21 February 1966. Sister locomotive No W24 *Calbourne* survives in preservation on the Isle of Wight Steam Railway.
Marcus Eavis/Online Transport Archive

Above: As the driver and passengers of Ford Popular 790DYD, one of the ex-Great Western Railway '1366' class 0-6-0PT, No 1369, makes its way along Custom House Quay in Weymouth in 1960. A total of six of this small class were built at Swindon Works in 1934 and, with their short wheelbase and light axle loading, were ideal for use of dockside lines like the Harbour Tramway in Weymouth. A number, including No 1369, were fitted with bells – visible just in front of the cab below the pannier tank – and steam-heating apparatus for working the Channel Island boat trains to and from the Quay station. Withdrawn in November 1964, No 1369 is the only member of the class to survive in preservation. The Weymouth Harbour Tramway was opened by the GWR in 1865; regular timetabled services over the route ceased in 1987 although the last train over the route did not run until 2 May 1999. The line remains extant but currently out of use.
Charles Firminger/Bob Bridger Collection/Online Transport Archive

Above: The Hemyock line in Devon – the Culm Valley Light Railway – was an anachronistic survivor into the 1960s. Opened on 29 May 1876, the branch from Tiverton Junction was operated by the GWR from the outset, passing to British Railways (Western Region) on Nationalisation in 1948. The most profitable traffic on the line was the creamery – situated in the background of this 1960 view taken of Hemyock – with the milk being shipped out via mixed trains in six-wheel refrigerated wagons. The usual motive power in the last years of steam operation was one of the diminutive 0-4-2T of the '14xx' class built at Swindon between 1932 and 1936 as seen in this view. A total of 75 of the class were built for use primarily on branch-line passenger and freight services. By this date passenger services over the Hemyock branch were approaching the end; they ceased on 7 September 1963 and the remaining freight traffic was then handled by diesel locomotives. The final milk trains operated on 31 October 1975.
Charles Firminger/Bob Bridger Collection/Online Transport Archive

Above: Straddling the counties of Devon and Dorset, the Lyme Regis branch was a relatively late addition to the railway network, not being opened by the London & South Western Railway until 1903. Steeply graded and with sharp curves, the branch was long the haunt of the 4-4-2Ts designed by William Adams but limited investment in the 1950s saw the route able to handle more modern and heavier locomotives – such as this Ivatt-designed 2-6-2T No 41307 pictured at the terminus in 1961. The use of these locomotives on the line, which commenced in 1960, was destined to be short-lived as diesel multiple-units took over in late 1963. One of the numerous branch lines listed for closure in the Beeching report, passenger services over the line ceased on 29 November 1965. The station building at Lyme Regis was, however, to be preserved; constructed in wood, it was dismantled and rebuilt at Alresford on the preserved Mid-Hants Railway. *Marcus Eavis/Online Transport Archive*

Above: One of two narrow gauge lines in Wales to pass from the Great Western to British Railways (Western Region) in 1948 was the Welshpool & Llanfair; this 2ft 6in line opened on 4 April 1903 and provided a link through the Banwy valley from Llanfair Caereinion through to Welshpool, where it met the standard gauge line from Shrewsbury westwards to Aberystwyth. Although passenger services were withdrawn on 9 February 1931, freight continued for a further quarter century. By the mid-1950s, traffic was in decline and the decision was made to close the route completely; final freight services operated on 3 November 1956. This was not, however, the end of the story as a preservation society was established to take over the line. On the occasion of

the society's AGM in early 1962, one of the two original 0-6-0T locomotives supplied to the line by Manchester-based Beyer Peacock – No 822 *The Earl* – which had just been overhauled and returned to Welshpool was operated. It is seen here on the section that ran through the street from the main line junction northwards. When the lease for the railway was agreed between the preservation society and British Railways later in 1962, the section from the main line station to the future terminus of the preserved line at Raven Square was excluded and, following further stock movements in 1963, the section through Welshpool was formally abandoned and lifted.

Phil Tatt/Online Transport Archive

Left: Frederick Hawksworth's 'Modified Hall' class of 4-6-0 for the Great Western Railway first appeared in 1944 and a total of 71 were constructed between then and 1950. Worcester-allocated No 7920 *Coney Hall* – seen here passing through Swindon in ex-works condition with a freight in April 1963 – was built at Swindon Works in September 1950. Like many of the steam locomotives built in Britain after World War 2, No 7920 was destined to have a relatively short operational career; it was finally withdrawn in June 1965. Seven of the type have been preserved.

Phil Tatt/Online Transport Archive

Left: Relatively few railway lines in Kent and Sussex were to lose their passenger services as a result of the rationalisation of the railway industry following *The Reshaping of Britain's Railways* report of March 1963. One of those that did close, however, was the cross-country route from Three Bridges to Tunbridge Wells Central via East Grinstead Low Level. Passenger services over the western section were withdrawn on 2 January 1967. Some three years, in June 1963, earlier, Class M7 0-4-4T No 30053 is pictured at Grange Road, the first intermediate station to the east of Three Bridges, with an eastbound service. A total of 105 of this Dugald Drummond design were produced for the London & South Western Railway between 1897 and 1911; No 30053 was completed at Nine Elms Works in 1905 and was destined to be one of the last to remain in service. Withdrawn in May 1964, the locomotive was preserved, being based in the USA between 1967 and 1987. Following repatriation, the locomotive is now based on the Swanage Railway.
Phil Tatt/Online Transport Archive

Left: Standing in Talyllyn Junction station with a two-coach eastbound service is Ivatt-designed Class 2MT 2-6-0 No 46511. This was one of a class of 128 locomotives built between 1946 and 1953 that, with a light axle loading, were designed for use on cross-country and branch line use. Talyllyn Junction station was situated four miles east of Brecon; slightly to the east of the station was a triangular junction that linked the Brecon & Merthyr Railway, which opened on 1 May 1863, with the Mid-Wales Railway, which opened on 23 August 1864. Both of these railways passed to the Great Western in 1923 and thus to British Railways (Western Region) at Nationalisation in 1948. When recorded here, both routes were approaching their final days, with passenger services on both routes being withdrawn on 31 December 1962. Seven of the 2-6-0 design survive in preservation.
Charles Firminger/Bob Bridger Collection/Online Transport Archive

Right: Between 1951 and 1961 a total of 999
Standard locomotives were built by British Railways
to the designs of Robert A. Riddles. The single most
numerous class was the '9F' 2-10-0 of which 251
were completed between January 1954 and March
1960. Designed primarily for freight traffic and used
heavily, for example, on the iron ore trains from Tyne
Dock to Consett steel works, the type was also used
to a limited extent on passenger work, most notably
on the Somerset & Dorset Joint line from Bath to
Bournemouth. The last of the class – and also the
last steam locomotive built for BR – was No 92220,
which was completed at Swindon Works and was
named *Evening Star*; this was the only '9F' to
receive a name whilst in BR service. The locomotive
is seen here at Templecombe in August 1963. Like
the majority of the class, No 92220's operational
career was short, being withdrawn in March 1965.
Preserved as part of the National Collection, No
92220 is one of nine of the type to survive in
preservation.
Phil Tatt/Online Transport Archive

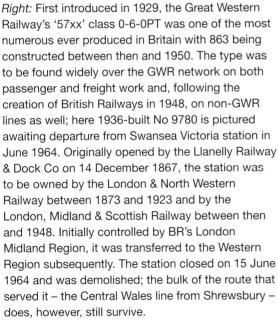

Right: First introduced in 1929, the Great Western
Railway's '57xx' class 0-6-0PT was one of the most
numerous ever produced in Britain with 863 being
constructed between then and 1950. The type was
to be found widely over the GWR network on both
passenger and freight work and, following the
creation of British Railways in 1948, on non-GWR
lines as well; here 1936-built No 9780 is pictured
awaiting departure from Swansea Victoria station in
June 1964. Originally opened by the Llanelly Railway
& Dock Co on 14 December 1867, the station was
to be owned by the London & North Western
Railway between 1873 and 1923 and by the
London, Midland & Scottish Railway between then
and 1948. Initially controlled by BR's London
Midland Region, it was transferred to the Western
Region subsequently. The station closed on 15 June
1964 and was demolished; the bulk of the route that
served it – the Central Wales line from Shrewsbury –
does, however, still survive.
Phil Tatt/Online Transport Archive

Above: On 27 July 1963 one of the diminutive 'Terrier' 0-6-0Ts built originally for the London, Brighton & South Coast Railway, No 32646, awaits departure from Hayling Island, the terminus of the branch from Havant. Designed by William Stroudley, the 'Terrier' class was built between 1872 and 1880 and built at Brighton Works. Although the first of the type had been withdrawn as long ago as 1901, a number survived into the British Railways era. Amongst their last duties – until the branch closed on 4 November 1963 – was on the Hayling Island branch where the wooden-built Langstone viaduct, between the main land and Hayling Island itself, precluded the use of heavier locomotives. No fewer than 10 of the class – including No 32646 (now restored as No W8 *Freshwater* on the Isle of Wight, where it operated in this guise for a period up to 1949) – have survived into preservation.
Roy Hobbs/Online Transport Archive

Above: On 10 September 1964, as Class 28xx 2-8-0 No 2895 backs out of Gloucester Central station tender first, the fireman of 'Hall' class No 6956 *Mottram Hall* attends to the coal in the tender whilst the locomotive receives water. The 'Hall' was one of the last of the unmodified Collett-designed 4-6-0s to be completed before the introduction of Hawksworth's 'Modified Hall' design. It was built at Swindon Works in March 1943. The '28xx' class was originally designed by George Jackson Churchward and introduced in 1903 – the first 2-8-0 freight type to be introduced to Britain – but No 2895 was one of 83 built to Charles Collett's modified design, the '2885' class, between 1938 and 1942. The modified locomotives were slightly heavier than the original and included side-window cabs. A number of the latter class were rebuilt as oil burners during the coal crisis of 1947 but all had reverted to coal by the end of the following year.
Marcus Eavis/Online Transport Archive

Left: In the late 1950s the Scottish Region of British Railways restored to their original liveries four historic locomotives that had originally been constructed by the pre-Grouping railway companies in the era before the creation of the 'Big Four' in 1923. For a number of years thereafter this quartet were used extensively on enthusiasts tours of the region, drawing large numbers to Scotland to witness them in action. Here two of the four – ex-Caledonian Railway 4-2-2 No 123 and ex-Great North of Scotland Railway No 49 *Gordon Highlander* – are seen at Carstairs, junction on the West Coast main line where the Caledonian's route to Edinburgh diverged from the main line to Glasgow Central, on 19 April 1965 during that Easter's programme of tours using the locomotives. No 123 was designed by Dugald Drummond and built by Neilson & Co of Glasgow in 1886. Constructed as a one-off for exhibition purposes, it was initially withdrawn for preservation in 1935; restored to service in 1958, it operated until the end of Scottish Region steam in 1967. Today, the locomotive is housed in the Glasgow Riverside Museum. No 49 was one of a class of eight Class F (later London & North Eastern Railway Class D40) 4-4-0s built during 1920 and 1921; withdrawn in June 1958, the locomotive was restored to a non-prototypical livery – it had been originally completed in lined black when new in 1920 – for special duties. It is now based at the Scottish Railway Museum at Bo'ness. The other two restored locomotives were North British Railway 4-4-0 No 256 *Glen Douglas* and Highland Railway 'Jones Goods' 4-6-0 No 103.
Charles Firminger/Bob Bridger Collection/Online Transport Archive

Left: Following the dieselisation of the East Coast main line north from King's Cross to Edinburgh, the Gresley-designed Class A4 Pacifics lost their historic role and a number were withdrawn as a result. A number, however, were to have an 'Indian Summer' operating on the express services from Glasgow to Aberdeen in Scotland. One of the class transferred to Scottish Region for this traffic was No 60024 *Kingfisher* which is seen here at Stirling in September 1965 with a service heading towards Glasgow. Although Stirling station itself opened in 1848, the station was completely rebuilt in 1916 to the design of James Miller and the resulting station buildings – which are still extant – are now listed Grade A by Historic Scotland. When recorded here, the 'A4'-operated Glasgow-Aberdeen services were themselves approaching their final months; the last of Gresley's classic streamlined design were taken out of service in September 1966.
Charles Firminger/Bob Bridger Collection/Online Transport Archive

Right: BR Standard Class 4 4-6-0 No 73113 *Lyonesse* stands in the up platform at Dorchester South in September 1966 with an eastbound departure heading towards Southampton. The station was originally opened by the Southampton & Dorchester Railway (later London & South Western Railway) on 1 June 1847 as a terminus; its alignment was based on plans to extend the line west towards Exeter. However, the line was extended south-westwards to Weymouth, with the southbound platform built on the new through route opening – following an accident – in 1878. Prior to that date, both up and down services had to reverse either into or out of the original station and, for services towards Southampton and London, this process continued until 1970 when a new eastbound platform was constructed on the through line. No 73113 was one of a class of 172 locomotives designed for mixed traffic work constructed between April 1951 and May 1957 at either Derby or Doncaster works. Following the withdrawal of the old 'King Arthur' class, a number of the Southern Region-based locomotives – including No 73113 – received the names previously used on the withdrawn locomotives from 1959 onwards.
Marcus Eavis/Online Transport Archive

Above: Following its withdrawal by British Railways in January 1963, Class A3 4-6-2 No 60103 *Flying Scotsman* was acquired for preservation by the late Alan Pegler. Widely regarded as one of Britain's most famous steam locomotives – and the oldest of Sir Nigel Gresley's designs of Pacific for the London & North Eastern to survive – BR had originally decided to scrap the locomotive and an appeal to raise funds for its preservation – £3,000 – had failed. Restored to LNER livery as No 4472, the locomotive was to operate steam specials on the main line until 1969 – after the last timetabled main-line services had operated – as Pegler had a contract to permit such operation until 1972. In 1966, in order to circumvent the reduction in watering facilities as steam traction was withdrawn, Pegler acquired a second tender and the locomotive with its two tenders are seen here awaiting departure from Norwich with a special in 1967. In 1969, No 4472 headed across to North America for an ill-fated tour; it was not to return to the UK until 1973.

Harry Luff/Online Transport Archive

Right: Although the north-west of England was destined to be the last centre of steam operation on British Railways, the last main line over which steam was dominant was that from London Waterloo to Bournemouth and Weymouth. Steam operation over the South Region main line ceased in July 1967 and, shortly before the end, the driver of Oliver Bulleid-designed rebuilt 'West Country' No 34025 *Whimple* awaits the right away from Waterloo with a down service. A total of 110 of Bulleid's light Pacific type – the 'West Country' and 'Battle of Britain' classes – were completed between 1945 and 1951. As built, the locomotives were fitted with air-smoothed casing and incorporated a number of novel features. However, these caused problems and, from 1957, 60 of the class – including No 34025 in October 1957 – were rebuilt with modified valve gear and casing. A number of the type – both rebuilt and unrebuilt – but not No 34025 survive in preservation.
Marcus Eavis/Online Transport Archive

Opposite left: Although main-line steam operation on British Railways ceased in August 1968, that was not to be the end of steam traction on the national network as it continued to be used on the 1ft 11½in gauge Vale of Rheidol line until the 11¾-mile long branch was privatised in 1989. Initially proposed in the late 19th century, the line from Aberystwyth to Devil's Bridge opened for freight traffic in August 1902 and to passenger services four months later. Although the freight traffic never reached the level anticipated by the line's promoters, the route became a successful tourist route and, unlike other Welsh narrow gauge lines, retained its passenger services. Acquired by the Great Western Railway in 1923, following the Grouping of the smaller railways into the so-called 'Big Four', the line received considerable investment from its new owners. This included the construction of three new 2-6-2Ts during 1923 and 1924; the last of this trio – No 9 *Prince of Wales* – is seen here on 12 September 1967 taking water at Aberffrwd.
John Worley/Online Transport Archive

Above: Although the ex-London & South Western main line from London Waterloo to Bournemouth and Weymouth was the last major main line to see its passenger services steam hauled in Britain, the last major centre of steam operation was in the north-west of England particularly on the main line north Crewe towards Carlisle. It was over the climb to Shap on British Railways (London Midland Region) that steam had its swansong until August 1968. In September the previous year, one of Sir William Stanier's classic 'Black Five' 4-6-0s – No 45349 (built by Sir W. G. Armstrong Whitworth & Co Ltd in May 1937) – is seen on a southbound freight having just passed the summit at Shap. The fireman will, at this point, be relaxing after the hard climb from Penrith – some 10 miles at up to 1 in 125. By this date No 45349 was approaching the end of its career; it was withdrawn two months later.
John Worley/Online Transport Archive

Above: In 1955 British Railways launched its Modernisation Plan; this envisaged the replacement of steam traction by diesel and electric as soon as it was practicable. As a result of significant closures in the 1960s, main-line steam operation came to an end on the BR network much earlier than originally planned and resulted in many steam locomotives built during the 1950s having a working life of less than a decade. On 11 August 1968 BR ran the 'Fifteen Guinea Special' from Liverpool Lime Street to Carlisle and return; this was the last steam-hauled main-line passenger train to be operated by BR with a ban on steam operation being introduced the following day. Four locomotives were used on the service; these included two of William Stanier's 'Black Five' class 4-6-0s – Nos 44871 and 44781 – that double-headed the return working from Carlisle to Manchester Victoria. The pair are seen here on that fateful day at Spring Vale. Of the four locomotives used that day, all bar No 44781 were to be preserved; the other two were another 'Black Five', No 45110, and one of the 'Britannia' class Pacifics, No 70013 *Oliver Cromwell*.
Alan Murray-Rust/Online Transport Archive

Right: Although largely electrified, London Transport (LT) had a small fleet of steam locomotives for use on engineering and ballast trains on the lines above ground. By the late 1950s the existing locomotives, inherited from the Metropolitan Railway in 1933, were life-expired and, with the planned programme of work, LT sought replacements. With the rapid reduction of BR's steam fleet, it was decided to acquire a number of 0-6-0PTs that were surplus to requirements on Western Region. In all, LT acquired 12 of the '57xx' class, originally designed by Charles Collett and built between 1929 and 1950, between 1956 and 1963. One of these, repainted into LT maroon, was L89, which is seen here at Watford during the summer of 1968; this had originally been Great Western Railway No 5775 and had been built at Swindon in September 1929. The last of the type were withdrawn from LT service in 1971, making them the last main-line steam locomotives in operation in Great Britain (other than a handful that were in industrial use). No L89 was one of six of the type sold to LT ultimately to be preserved.
Harry Luff/Online Transport Archive

Above: In 1939 and 1940 the Great Southern Railways introduced a class of three 4-6-0s designed by Edgar Bredin and built at Inchicore. Nos 800-02 were the largest and most powerful steam locomotive ever built for operation in Ireland; in addition, they were also the only express steam passenger locomotives built in Ireland after the creation of the Free State. The type – of which five were originally planned – was designed to operate on the Dublin to Cork main line, but fuel shortages during the war allied to post-war dieselisation meant that they never fulfilled their potential and, by the late 1950s, were largely redundant. Here the first of the trio –

No 800 *Maeve* – is seen standing outside the shed at Thurles on 4 June 1961; withdrawn shortly thereafter, the locomotive was stored in the shed here until it was acquired for preservation. Today, No 800 is on display in the Ulster Folk & Transport Museum at Cultra; Nos 801 and 802 were both scrapped in the early 1960s.
Roy Hobbs/Online Transport Archive

Right: The last steam locomotives acquired by the Dublin & South Eastern Railway (DSER) were two 2-6-0s produced by Beyer Peacock & Co in 1922 to the designs of the last chief mechanical engineer of the railway – G. H. Wild – to haul the heavy freight trains on the main line from Dublin to Wexford. Built in 1922, the locomotives were delivered during the Irish civil war and so were stored on delivery for a brief period by the Great Northern Railway (Ireland) (GNR[I]) in Belfast. The duo finally entered service in 1923. The DSER was to become part of the Great Southern Railway on 1 January 1925, with the newly enlarged railway becoming known as the Great Southern Railways. Following the Transport Act of 1944, the railway was taken over by Córas Iompair Éireann (CIÉ; Irish Transport Authority) on 1 January 1945. One of the two – No 461 (which was later to be preserved) – is seen here at Dungarvan on 6 June 1961.
Charles Firminger/Bob Bridger Collection/Online Transport Archive

Above: On 9 June 1961 Class SG3 0-6-0 No 14 is pictured shunting at Dublin Amiens Street station. A total of 15 of the type were built by Beyer Peacock & Co during 1920 and 1921 to the design of George T. Glover, the chief mechanical engineer of the GNR(I) between 1912 and 1933. On the division of that railway's assets between the Ulster Transport Authority (UTA) and Córas Iompair Éireann in 1958, seven passed to the latter and eight to the former. All of the CIÉ examples were withdrawn by the end of 1967. Amiens Street station – the busiest in Ireland – was originally opened as simply Dublin on 29 November 1844 by the Dublin & Drogheda Railway; it gained the suffix Amiens Street in 1854 and was considerably extended during the second half of the 19th century. In 1966 – on the 50th anniversary of the Easter Rising – the station was renamed Dublin Connolly after James Connolly, one of the leaders of the rising who was executed in May 1916. *Charles Firminger/Bob Bridger Collection/Online Transport Archive*

Above: Pictured on the causeway on the approach to Dungarvan in October 1962 is CIE No 249 with the 1pm goods from Waterford. The section of the former Great Southern & Western line from Losmore to Waterford opened on 12 August 1878 and the entire line, from Waterford to Mallow, closed completely on 27 March 1967 (although the section to the east of Dungarvan – from Ballinacourty to Waterford – was reopened between 3 April 1970 and 28 July 1982 by CIE for freight traffic). There were four members of Robert Coey-designed class of 0-6-0 – Nos 249-52 – that were built at Inchicore in 1903 primarily for the operation of freight trains. All four were withdrawn by the end of 1964 with none surviving into preservation.
Roy Hobbs/Online Transport Archive

Opposite above: Ex-Midland Great Western Railway Class L (and Great Southern Railways Class J19) 0-6-0 No 610 stands outside the shed at Ballaghadereen in October 1962. The 10-mile-long branch from Kilfree Junction to Ballaghadereen opened on 2 November 1874 and was to survive until all services were withdrawn on 4 February 1963. The first 10 of the design were built in 1876 with a further 18 being delivered between 1886 and 1889; the following decade saw the original locomotives rebuilt, to become Class Lm (later Class J18) whilst 17 of the later batch passed to Córas Iompair Éireann when the future nationalised railway was established by the Transport Act of 1944, initially as a private company. The majority of the survivors were withdrawn by 1957 with the last two being withdrawn in 1965.
Roy Hobbs/Online Transport Archive

Opposite below: Recorded shunting at Omagh during the summer of 1964 is Ulster Transport Authority 0-6-0 No 43. This was one of five members of the 'SG' class constructed by Manchester-based Beyer Peacock & Co Ltd in 1913 to the design of Charles Clifford for the GNR(I). A further five similar locomotives were delivered in 1915 and a final batch of five during 1924 and 1925. The last 10 locomotives were designated Class SG2. Two of the original quintet were taken over by the UTA in 1958; No 43 had originally been GNR(I) No 137 (renumbered 175 almost from new) and both remained in service until 1965. The line from Portadown via Omagh to Londonderry closed completely on 15 February 1965, the route from Omagh to Clones having been closed on 1 October 1957.
Marcus Eavis/Online Transport Archive

Opposite above: Heading south towards Adelaide, on the outskirts of Belfast, with a UTA service from Great Victoria Street towards Lisburn during the summer of 1964 is ex-GNR(I) Class S 4-4-0 No 60. The line from Lisburn to Belfast originally opened, courtesy of the Ulster Railway, on 12 August 1839. Following the Northern Ireland government's acquisition of the GNR(I) lines in Ulster, most of the network was closed in the late 1950s; the line through Lisburn – part of the main line to Dublin – however was to survive and remains operational. Designed by G. T. Glover, No 60 – which had originally carried the name *Slieve Donard* and been numbered 172 by the GNR(I) – was one of a class of five locomotives built by Beyer Peacock in 1913. All were rebuilt during 1938 and 1939, and, following the division of the GNR(I)'s assets between the UTA and CIE in 1958, was one of two of the class to be taken over by the former. No 60 was withdrawn in 1965; the other UTA locomotive, No 61, succumbed the previous year. One of the CIE examples, GNR(I) No 171 *Slieve Gullion,* is preserved.
Marcus Eavis/Online Transport Archive

Opposite below: Based upon the work of William Stanier in England, the 'W' class 2-6-0s constructed for the Northern Counties Committee was designed by the NCC's Chief Mechanical Engineer H. P. Stewart. Introduced in 1933, primarily for express passenger work out of Belfast York Road station, a total of 15 – Nos 90-104 – were constructed at the company's York Road Works. No 91 *The Bush* is pictured here on shed during the summer of 1964 towards the end of its life; all of the class were withdrawn by the end of the following year and were scrapped.
Marcus Eavis/Online Transport Archive

Above: When Northern Ireland Railways was created in 1966, it inherited 23 steam locomotives from the Ulster Transport Authority. The majority of these were 2-6-4Ts originally supplied to the Northern Counties Committee between 1946 and 1950. Designed by George Ivatt and built at Derby Works, the locomotives – Nos 1-10 and 50-57 – were designated Class WT and much of their later work was operating spoil trains from the Blue Circle cement works at Magheramorne to Greencastle to aid the construction of a motorway. Each train consisted of 20 hopper wagons carrying some 600 tonnes. No 50 is seen at Carrickfergus in March 1968 on one of these spoil trains. This locomotive was modified in December 1962 when it received the boiler from a withdrawn 2-6-0. The last Class WT operated on 22 October 1970, making the type the last steam locomotives in regular service on the main line in the British Isles. One of the class – No 4 – was preserved on withdrawal.
Harry Luff/Online Transport Archive

Right: On 19 August 1960, passengers alight at Kirk Michael station on the former Manx Northern Railway line between St John's and Ramsey. The 3ft 0in route through Kirk Michael originally opened on 23 September 1879; operated from November 1880 by the MNR, the company was to merge with the Isle of Man Railway in 1905. The St John's to Ramsey line was finally to lose its passenger services on 6 September 1968. The train is headed by No 5 *Mona*; this was one of two 2-4-0Ts supplied by Beyer Peacock to the Isle of Man Railway in 1874 for the opening of the line to Port Erin. Reboilered in 1946, No 5 was taken out of service at the end of the 1969 season and, 50 years on, remains in store and in a poor condition.
Les Folkard/Online Transport Archive

Left: On the same day No 8 *Fenella* stands outside the shed at St John's. Built by Beyer Peacock in 1894, the locomotive is seen in the Indian Red livery that it carried between 1946 and 1965. Unique amongst the railway's first nine locomotives, No 8 was fitted with a larger diameter boiler; this, in theory, gave the locomotive about the same power output as the later – 'medium boiler' – examples, although this was not wholly successful. Allocated for many years to the Ramsey section, No 8 was withdrawn at the end of 1969; preserved a decade later, following restoration the locomotive was again operational – this time between Port Erin and Douglas – for a period during the first decade of the 21st century and is, at the time of writing, again part of the operational fleet.
Les Folkard/Online Transport Archive

Above: Built by Beyer Peacock of Manchester in 1905 for the Isle of Man Railway, 0-4-2T No 11 *Maitland* is pictured about to reverse on to its train at Douglas station in this view. The locomotive had recently received a new boiler when recorded and this work ensured that it was operational throughout the decade, an era when the future of the steam railway was under considerable doubt. The first section of the 3ft 0in gauge system – from Douglas to Peel – opened on 1 July 1873, to be followed by the line from Douglas to Port Erin on 1 August 1974. To serve Douglas, the railway eventually constructed a substation brick-built station; this building still survives and can be seen beyond the buffer stops in this view. No 11 remains part of the current owner's fleet.

John Worley/Online Transport Archive

Above: On 13 August 1967 Isle of Man Railway No 12 *Hutchinson* passes over the level crossing at Quarter Bridge, to the west of Douglas, with a southbound train from either Peel or Ramsey. Built by Beyer Peacock in 1908, the 2-4-0T was named after William Hutchinson, one of the railways directors and a local politician. The locomotive, now restored to her condition from the 1950s, remains operational on the surviving section of the railway from Douglas to Port Erin. The crossing at Quarter Bridge was situated just north of the junction where the line towards Peel and Ramsey split from the route west to Port Erin. By the early 1960s, the finances of the railway company had seriously deteriorated and the surviving network was closed at the end of the 1965 season. Leased by the Marquess of Ailsa in 1967, services were restored although passenger services over the Peel route and that from St John's to Ramsey ceased at the end of the 1968 season, on 6 September. Ailsa's lease to operate the remaining section of the railway expired at the end of 1971 and, following several years of struggle, the surviving section from Douglas to Port Erin was Nationalised in 1978. The track through Quarter Bridge to Peel and to Ramsey was lifted during 1974 and 1975.
Alan Murray-Rust/Online Transport Archive

Below: Viewed looking towards the east, an Isle of Man Railway service approaches Crosby station from Douglas on 31 August 1968. Situated to the west of a level crossing, Crosby station provided one of the passing loops on the single-track route from Douglas north to Peel. The station, which lacked raised platforms, opened with the line on 1 July 1873. Like the remainder of the Douglas to Peel route, it was approaching its final days when recorded here: it closed completely on 7 September 1968. The track was lifted during 1974 and 1975 and the former railway route is now a footpath and cycleway.
John McCann/Online Transport Archive

Right: During World War 1, the Railway Operating Division – part of the British army's Royal Engineers and established in 1915 – acquired a significant number of steam locomotives from both Britain and elsewhere to support the war effort. One of the principal overseas suppliers of locomotives was the US-based Baldwin Locomotive Works. Amongst this company's products supplied to the Western Front during the war were 70 4-6-0s; following the cessation of hostilities, these were sold to the Société Nationale des Chemins de Fer Belges (SNCB), where they were to become Class 40. No 40.011 is seen here in September 1962; none of the type survive in preservation.
Frank Hunt/LRTA (London Area) Collection/Online Transport Archive

Right: Built between 1935 and 1938, the 35-strong Class 1 Pacifics were designed for the operation of express passenger services of SNCB. With semi-streamlined casing and four cylinders, the width of the firebox was so great that it required two firehole doors. With a total weight of some 124 tonnes and an axle load of just under 24 tonnes, the class was the heaviest Pacific type to see service in Europe. Here No 1.005 is seen at Mons in 1961 shortly before withdrawal; the last of the type were withdrawn the following year and No 1.002 survives in preservation.
Les Folkard/Online Transport Archive

Right: Following the Treaty of Versailles in 1919, Germany was required to transfer a significant number of steam locomotives as reparations to a number of other countries. These included 627 of the Prussian Class P8 4-6-0 designed by Robert Garde; of these 168 were passed to SNCB where they were – after the 1931 renumbering – to become Nos 64.001-168. In this undated view No 64.123 is pictured awaiting departure from Antwerp station. All of the Class 64s were withdrawn by the end of 1967; one of the type – No 64.045 – has been preserved although a spurious No 64.169 has been restored to main line operational condition following the acquisition of a Romanian example in 2002. Antwerp Central station dates rebuilt between 1895 and 1905; more recently, the station has undergone considerable rebuilding to be converted from a terminus to a through station for high-speed services.
Geoffrey Morant/Online Transport Archive

Above: The Class T16 0-10-T of Prussian State Railways was first introduced in 1905 and, between then and 1913, 343 were constructed for operation in Prussia along with a further 12 for the Kaiserliche Generaldirektion der Eisenbahnen in Elsaß-Lothringen (EL; Imperial Railways of Alsace-Lorraine [an area that, since 1870, had been under German rule]). Following World War 1, 17 of the class passed to SNCB as wartime reparations. In 1913 a modified version – the T16.1 0-10-0T – first emerged; a total of 1,242 of these locomotives were constructed by 1924. Of these, 36 passed to SNCB after World War 1, resulting in SNCB operating 53 ex-Prussian 0-10-0Ts, which were designated as Class 98. Here No 98.015 is seen at work in Liège in 1961. None of the Belgian examples survive.
Les Folkard/Online Transport Archive

Opposite above: Recorded at Vervier in April 1962 is 0-8-0 Class 81 No 81.122. The most numerous type of steam locomotive in Belgium in the years after World War 2 – with 532 in service immediately after the end of the war – the type originated as the Prussian Class G8.1; this was designed by Robert Garbe and built in large numbers between 1913 and 1921. Derived from the earlier Class G8, the type had larger boilers and increased tractive effort. The resulting higher axle loading meant that the type was capable of hauling heavier trains but at the cost of being restricted to main-line use only as a result of the weight.
Phil Tatt/Online Transport Archive

Opposite below: Introduced in 1904, 436 Class 53 (originally Class 23) 0-8-0Ts were constructed for Chemins de fer de l'État Belge (SNCB/NMBS from 1 September 1926) between then and 1926. Designed primarily for use as shunters, the type was seen widely across the Belgian railway network; the last were withdrawn by the end of 1966 and one – No 53.320 – is preserved. Here No 53.085 is seen undertaking shunting duties.
Marcus Eavis/Online Transport Archive

Above: A total of 300 Class 29 2-8-0s were built for SNCB by three North American locomotive builders – the Montreal Locomotive Works, the American Locomotive Co (Alco) and the Canadian Locomotive Co – during 1945 and 1946. They were supplied to Belgium as part of as a precursor to the post-war European Recovery Program – better known as the Marshall Plan – with a design that was based upon that adopted for the 2-8-0s supplied to the US Army during the war. No 29.119 is seen here at Verviers Central on 5 October 1964. Sister locomotive No 29.013 was to haul the official last steam train in Belgium; now preserved, No 29.013 is the only example of the type to survive intact (a second still survives as a stationary boiler and a third was cut-up as recently as 2002).
Frank Hunt/LRTA (London Area) Collection/Online Transport Archive

Above: Apart from SNCB, Belgium also had a second national network of predominantly metre-gauge lines that belonged to the Société Nationale des Chemins de Fer Vicinaux (SNCV; Vicinal Railways). This company operated both steam and electric railways and tramways. One of its three standard gauge lines was that which linked Poulseur to Trooz via Sprimont to the south of Liège. The section from Poulseur to Sprimont, authorised on 9 December 1887, was opened in two states by the end of 1888. Extending for just over 5¾ miles, the line was designed to serve the local stone quarries. The line was extended to Trooz during the first decade of the 20th century, with the final section opening on 22 January 1908. This resulted in the line reaching its maximum length: just under 14 miles. The SNCV took over ownership in 1920. Never a very profitable line, passenger services were withdrawn in 1937 at which stage the Sprimont-Trooz section closed completely. Stone traffic, however, continued; with the aid of a major contract to supply material for dyke building work in The Netherlands the Sprimont-Poulseur section survived until final closure in 1965. For the operation of the line, three 0-6-0T Class 11 locomotives were supplied; these were Nos 800-02 and all survived until the closure of the line in 1965. This view records one of the trio at the quarries at Sprimont in 1964, towards the end of the line's life. Although none of these three locomotives survive, similar Class 10 No 808 – built for the line from Dolhain to Goe and Membach – is preserved.
Phil Tatt/Online Transport Archive

Above: Class 141F 2-8-2 No 141F218 recorded in mid-1959; the side view shows to good effect the combined length of the locomotive and eight-wheel tender (some 74ft 7¼in). The first 2-8-2s produced for operation in France were supplied to the Compagnie du Chemin de Fer Paris-Lyon-Méditerranée (PLM; the Paris-Lyon-Mediterranean Railway) in 1914. A further batch, supplied by Baldwin Locomotive Works, followed during World War 1 as the company needed additional locomotives but domestic production was concentrated on the war effort. In 1918 the first of the Class 141C was produced; between then and 1927 a total of 490 were completed with a further 180 during 1933 and 1934. With the creation of Société Nationale des Chemins de Fer Français (SNCF; French National Railways) in 1938, PLM was absorbed and from 1942 onwards the '141C' class underwent various modifications, being reclassified as 141D, 141E or 141F as a result. A total of 182 of the class were modified to become Class 141F; these modifications included the smoke deflectors, as used on the '141E', along with work on the front bissel axle in order to permit a higher maximum speed of 105km/h. One of the Class 141Fs survives: No 141F282 is preserved at Mulhouse.
Online Transport Archive

Right: On 2 September 1960 Class 231G 4-6-2 No 231G87 awaits departure from Troyes on the Paris to Mulhouse line with a southbound service. PLM was the single largest user of Pacific locomotives prior to the creation of SNCF with a total of 462 being constructed from 1909 onwards; from 1917 onwards a number of the earlier types were modified. The Nos 6301-480 series was first introduced in 1921; these were to become Nos 231D1-180 in 1925. That same year saw Nos 231D181-230 completed to be followed, during 1931 and 1932, by Nos 231F231-80, which were an improved version of the '231D'. The locomotives were supplied by a number of manufacturers; No 231G87 was one of a batch of 50 – Nos 6361-410 – supplied by Saint-Chamond (as the builder Compagnie des forges et aciéries de la marine et d'Homécourt is better known after its main workshops). From the mid-1930s through to 1949 the majority of both types underwent further modification to become Class 231G.
John McCann/Online Transport Archive

Right: On 4 June 1961 Class 231E No 231E17 stands at Calais Maritime station with the 'Flèche d'Or' ('Golden Arrow') working to Paris. The service was a luxury boat train that provided a link between London Victoria to Dover and from Calais to Paris. The French section of the Pullman service was introduced in 1926 whilst the English section was launched on 15 May 1929 contemporaneously with the introduction of a new first-class only ferry – the *Canterbury* – although the 1930s saw the service modified. Suspended during World War 2, it was revived on 15 April 1946. Over the post-war years the service altered but the growth of air traffic, and the consequent decline in passengers wanting luxury rail travel between Paris and London, saw the service withdrawn in 1972. No 231E17 was one of 20 four-cylinder compounds rebuilt by André Chapelon in 1934 from older locomotives built originally for the Compagnie du Paris-Orléans; these were to become Compagnie du Nord Nos 2.1171-90 and SNCF Nos 231E1-20. A further 28 were built new to a similar design during 1936 and 1937.
John McCann/Online Transport Archive

Right: Between 1908 and 1927 the Chemins de Fer de l'Est acquired 134 4-6-0s, Nos 3147-3280, from four manufacturers. The locomotives were modified between 1932 and 1946 by the addition of SNCF feedwater heaters, being reclassified from Class 230J to 230K, becoming eventually Nos 230K147-280. In 1948 12 of the type were rebuilt in streamlined form and converted to operate as oil-fired locomotives on light high-speed services running between Paris and Strasbourg. One of the non-streamlined locomotives – No 230K256 – is pictured here about to depart from Delle, the last station in France on the line from Belfort to Berne, on 16 June 1961.
John McCann/Online Transport Archive

Above: Pictured across the Belgian border at Mons on 14 August 1961 is Class 230D 4-6-0 No 230D105. Between 1908 and 1912 the Chemins de Fer du Nord, one of the five main constituents of SNCF in 1938, took delivery of 150 locomotives – Nos 3.513-662 – that were designed by Gaston du Bousquet, the railway's Chief of Motive Power – that adopted the de Glehn method of compounding which Bousquet had improved based on experience with the early prototypes supplied to the railway by Société Alsacienne de Constructions Mécaniques (SACM). The class was subsequently modified with piston valve cylinders and Lemaître blast-pipes. The surviving locomotives were to become SNCF Nos 230D1-149. Withdrawal of the class commenced post-war in 1955 and all had been take out of service by 1969. One of the class – No 230D9 – survives in preservation.
Les Folkard/Online Transport Archive

Above: Pictured departing from Paris Saint-Lazare station in May 1964 is SNCF 2-8-2T No 141TD112. The 40-strong class originated with the Chemins de Fer de l'Etat and was introduced in 1932; production was split equally between Schneider et Cie and Batignolles-Chatillon. The type was designed primarily for suburban services into and out of Paris. Saint-Lazare station – one of the six major terminal stations that serves the French capital – handles train services that serve the area to the north-west of the city and first opened in 1837 slightly to the north-west of its current position; the current building – built in a French chateau style – was designed by Juste Lisch. When recorded here, the inner suburban lines were served by third-rail electric trains; during the later 1960s, these were replaced by services operated by 25kV overhead trains.
Les Folkard/Online Transport Archive

Above: Although born in Britain, Alfred de Glehn is best known for his work in developing the type of four-cylinder compound steam locomotives that bore his name. As an engineer at the Société Alsacienne de Constructions Mécaniques (SACM) he designed his first compound locomotives in the last decade of the 19th century, working closely with Gaston du Bousquet, the chief engineer of the Chemins de Fer du Nord. In 1908 the first of the company's 4-6-0 design that would become SNCF Class 230D in 1938 was constructed. Between then and 1911 a total of 150 of the class were constructed; of these 149 passed to SNCF with the penultimate built – No 3.661 – having been destroyed by bombing at Romescamps in 1917 during World War 1. Designed for high-speed express passenger duties, the type survived on main-line services between Paris Gare du Nord and Beauvais and Tréport until the mid-1960s. Recorded at Calais in June 1966 is the last of the type in service, No 230D125; this was the last of a batch manufactured by Herschel in 1911. Two of the class – Nos 230D9 and 230D116 – have been preserved.
John Worley/Online Transport Archive

Above: Between 1891 and 1925 a network of some 266 route miles of metre gauge railway was constructed to serve Brittany by the Chemins de Fer de l'Ouest. Known as the Réseau Breton, the lines were constructed to be converted to standard gauge at a later date, if required. Although passenger services were withdrawn in 1939, the requisitioning of the replacement services in the war led to their reinstatement whilst construction of the Atlantic Wall along the Breton coast resulted in an increase in freight traffic during the wartime years. After the war passenger services were again progressively withdrawn and all of the surviving metre gauge sections were closed finally on 9 April 1967.

Pictured at Loudéac the month before closure with a freight service is No 41; this 0-6-6-0T Mallet had been constructed by Corpet-Louvet of Paris in 1913. Originally built for the Chemins de Fer du Centre, it eventually reached the Réseau Breton in 1953 but was not used on the line until being rebuilt four years later. Loudéac was an intermediate station on the 81-mile route from Carhaix to La Brohinière; this opened from St Lubin-le-Vaublanc to Loudéac on 1 October 1904 and thence to La Brohinière on 12 August 1907.
Charles Firminger/Bob Bridger Collection/Online Transport Archive

Above: Although much of the Réseau Breton remained narrow gauge throughout its life, the section from Carhaix to Paimpol was converted to standard gauge. The line opened from Carhaix to Guingamp – a distance of 33 miles – on 24 September 1893 and was extended a further 23 miles from Guingamp to Paimpol on 14 August 1894. The Guingamp-Paimpol section was converted to mixed gauge, with standard gauge operation commencing over the route on 24 May 1924; in 1953 this section was converted to standard gauge only. The Guingamp to Carhaix section was closed on 14 February 1967, reopening as a standard gauge line

on 3 July 1967. Recorded in Guingamp station in March 1967 is 2-8-2T No 141TC1 awaiting departure with a service towards Paimpol. This was one of 20 locomotives built for the Chemins de Fer de l'État by Fives-Lille in 1923 primarily for suburban services serving the western suburbs of Paris. Following electrification of the suburban services serving Gare Saint-Lazare, the class was transferred to Brittany with the last being withdrawn in 1971. One of the type – No 141TC19 – was preserved.
Charles Firminger/Bob Bridger Collection/Online Transport Archive

Above: On 29 May 1967 SNCF 2-8-2 No 141R791 heads away from Cherbourg with a freight service. Based upon an American design of 'Mikado', a total of 1,340 of the class were ordered from a variety of North American manufacturers to help solve a significant shortage of motive power on the French railways in the period immediately after the end of World War 2. Supplied under the Lend-Lease programme, the first of the locomotives arrived in France in November 1945. Production was split between the US companies Lima, Baldwin and Alco and the Canadian suppliers, the Canadian Locomotive Co and the Montreal Locomotives Works. Although 1,340 were ordered, only 1,323 entered service as 17 were lost in April 1947 when the ship transporting them – the MV *Belpamela* – sank. No 141R791 was one of those constructed by the Pennsylvania-based Baldwin Locomotive Works. A significant number of the class, such as No 141R791, were constructed as oil-burners to reduce SNCF's demands for high quality coal – these were nicknamed *les goudronneuses* ('tar spraying machines') by the crews; this had the additional benefit of extending the range of the type. The last '141R' was taken out of service in October 1975; 12 of the type survive in preservation. *Les Folkard/Online Transport Archive*

Right: Gare de la Bastille in Paris originally opened in 1859 and was designed by François-Alexis Cendier for the Chemins de Fer de l'Est's route via Vincennes and Verneuil-l'Étang to Mulhouse. The station closed on 15 December 1969 following the decision to incorporate the Vincennes route into part of a new underground line and was to be demolished in 1984. The Opéra Bastille was built on the site of the station. Pictured awaiting departure from the station in July 1967 is No 141TB464. Designed by Louis Salomon for the CF de l'Est, 112 of this type of 2-8-2T were built between 1913 and 1917 for use on suburban services out of Paris. No 141TB464 was one of 30 supplied by Cail in 1914. The type had been transferred to the Vincennes line in 1962 following the electrification of the main Paris-Strasbourg route and, following the conversion of the Vincennes route to form part of RER line A, a number were reallocated for further work. The last were withdrawn in 1972 and two survive in preservation.
John Worley/Online Transport Archive

Above: Pictured light engine at Gray in July 1967 is Class 130B 2-6-0 No 130B476. This was one of 92 locomotives rebuilt by the Chemins de Fer de l'Est between 1909 and 1926 at its workshops at Épernay from older 0-6-0s. These were originally numbered between 30254 and 30766, becoming between Nos 130B254 and 130B766 upon the creation of SNCF in 1938. In the case of No 130B476 it was originally built in 1883 and was rebuilt at Épernay in 1922. The rebuilt locomotives were more powerful and economic than the original 0-6-0s and, with a low axle weight, were suitable for operation across the network on both passenger and freight traffic. Withdrawn following its last duty on 9 November 1970, No 130B476 was subsequently preserved – one of three of the type to survive – the locomotive is now based at Longueville.
John Worley/Online Transport Archive

Above: The photographer seems to have caught the attention of the footplate crew as 282 No 141C180 departs from Roche sur Yon with a freight on 9 September 1967. First introduced by the Chemins de Fer de l'Est in 1921, 250 of the type were built between then and 1923, with production divided between Schneider et Cie (190) and SACM with 60; No 141C280 was produced by the former in 1922. Designed for passenger and freight traffic, the class was used widely over the Chemins de Fer de l'Est network as well as that of the Chemins de Fer de l'Ouest. Originally designated as Class 141B when taken over by SNCF, modifications undertaken in the mid to late 1930s resulted in increased power with the locomotives being renumbered in the 141C series when work was completed. One of the class – No 141C100 – is preserved.

Charles Firminger/Bob Bridger Collection/Online Transport Archive

Above: Recorded blowing off at Calais Gare Maritime on 29 September 1967 is 4-6-2 four-cylinder compound No 231K82. Originally built for the Chemins de Fer de Paris à Lyon et à la Méditerranée (PLM) between 1909 and 1921, PLM had planned to rebuild the Class 231C locomotives but the work had not been undertaken by the date of the SNCF take-over in 1938 and a total of 86 were rebuilt between 1939 and 1949. The type had its four cylinders in line, with the high-pressure ones outside the frames, and had independent cut-off for the low- and high-pressure cylinders. Calais Gare Maritime was first opened in 1849 to provide a connection for passengers making use of the cross-channel ferries to England. Rebuilt in 1889, the station was to survive until 1995 when, following the opening of the Channel Tunnel, passenger services were cut back to terminate at Calais Ville station.
John Worley/Online Transport Archive

Above: Designed by Marc de Caso, the 72-strong Class 141TC was constructed originally for the Chemin de Fer du Nord for use on the company's suburban services out of Paris. Constructed by a number of manufacturers between 1932 and 1935, the 2-8-2Ts used the same boilers as the company's earlier class of Pacific (SNCF Class 231C). Two of the type – No 141TC7, built by Société Alsacienne de Constructions Mécaniques in 1933, and No 141TC28, built by Société Franco-Belge in the same year – are pictured here awaiting departure from Paris Gare du Nord during the summer of 1968. The last of the type were taken out of service on 12 December 1970 with the completion of the electrification of the suburban services over which they operated. One of the class – No 141TC51 – survives in preservation.
Harry Luff/Online Transport Archive

Above: During 1948 and 1949 the Société Nationale des Chemins de Fer Luxembourgeois (CFL) acquired 21, Nos 5501-21, 2-10-0s that had been constructed by the Vienna-based Lokomotivfabrik Floridsdorf. Based upon the wartime 'Kriegslok' Class 42 design introduced to Deutsche Reichsbahn in 1943, 76 of the type were built in Austria after the war. Here No 5506 can be seen departing from the station serving Luxembourg city with a southbound passenger service. Situated between Belgium, France and Germany, the railways of Luxembourg provide connections into all three of the neighbouring countries and the first section – south from Luxembourg through Bettembourg to the French border – opened on 11 August 1859. The link to the Belgian border via Kleinbettingen followed on 15 September 1859 and that to Germany via Wasserbillig on 29 August 1861.
Marcus Eavis/Online Transport Archive

Above: A second view of one of the Austrian-built 2-10-0s sees No 5513 light engine. Below the locomotive number can be seen three coloured dots; that on the left indicates water treatment, that in the centre the percentage of white metal in the bearings and that on the right that it has a steel firebox. Although CFL, which was 51% owned by the government with the other half being shared between the Belgian and French governments, was established on 17 April 1946, it did not assume control of the lines in Luxembourg until June 1947. By the mid-1950s work was in hand on the electrification of the network, with the first electric services operating on the line from Kleinbettingen to Bettembourg via Luxembourg City on 28 September 1956. The Class 55s were withdrawn by the mid-1960s with one – No 5519 – being retained for preservation.
Marcus Eavis/Online Transport Archive

Opposite left: One of the predecessors to CFL was the Compagnie de Chemins de Fer Prince-Henri (the Prince Henry Railway Co; named after the then Lieutenant-governor of Luxembourg) which was founded in 1869 to construct a main line from Esch-Alzette to Steinfort with associated branches. The first sections opened on 1 August 1873 but the company was soon in financial trouble and, in 1879, was reconstituted as the Société Luxembourgeoise des Minières et Chemins de Fer de Prince Henri (the Luxembourg Company of Mines and Railways of Prince Henry). Between 1914 and 1918 the company took delivery of 13 powerful 2-6-2Ts – Class L – that would become CFL Class 35. Built by Maschinenbau-Gesellschaft Karlsruhe (Nos 251-56) and Arnold Jung Lokomotivfabrik (Nos 257-63), the locomotives were allocated CFL Nos 3501-13 and this view records the last of the batch, which was new in 1918, at Pétange in April 1961. Two of the class – Nos 256 and 259 – were withdrawn in Austria and Germany during the late 1940s with the remaining 11 withdrawn by CFL between 1957 and 1963.
Geoffrey Morant/Online Transport Archive

Above: Alongside the Class 55 2-10-0s, CFL also acquired a further 20 2-10-0s based upon the German Class 52; these were to become Nos 5601-20. The first 10 of these were part of a batch of 100 built in Belgium immediately after the war; the remaining 90 became SNCB Class 26. The next 10 were constructed by the Elsässische Maschinenbau-Gesellschaft Grafenstaden (Alsatian Engineering Company in Grafenstaden) in 1947. Here one of the Belgian-built examples – No 5609 – is pictured awaiting its next duty in the city. None of the CFL locomotives survive in preservation; likewise, all 90 of the batch that operated in Belgium have been scrapped as well. However, a similar locomotive operated in Poland was acquired and has been restored as SNCB No 26.101.
Charles Firminger/Bob Bridger Collection/Online Transport Archive

Right: The Rotterdamsche Tramweg Maatschappij (RTM; Rotterdam Tramway Co) operated a network of narrow gauge (3ft 6in) lines to the remote communities to the south-west of Rotterdam. The first section opened in May 1898 with the last operating in February 1966. The section from Spijkenisse to Oostvoorne opened on 1 September 1906 and, with a link to the beach at Oostvoorne, it was to provide a useful boost to the local economy. The line was extended slightly in 1950 but was finally to be withdrawn on 23 September 1965. In all the company operated 58 steam locomotives during its life; the last three – including No 56 seen at Oostvoorne during an enthusiasts' tour during 1961 – were supplied by Orestein & Koppel in 1920. No 56 along with No 57 and two other steam locomotives have been preserved.
Les Folkard/Online Transport Archive

Above: The origins of the Class 74 2-6-0T lay with the Preußische Staatseisenbahnen (Prussian State Railways) Class T12, itself a superheated version of the earlier T11. Four prototypes were built in 1902 but it was not until 1905 that series production commenced with examples also being sold to the state railways in Alsace-Lorraine, to the Lübeck-Büchener Eisenbahn (Lübeck-Büchener Railway) and to the Halberstadt-Blankenburger Eisenbahn (Halberstadt-Blankenburger Railway). The final batch of 40, built by Borsig, were constructed in 1921. Primarily used on the suburban lines around Berlin that were later electrified as part of the Stadtbahn between 1924 and 1929, the class was then largely used on shunting duties as well as short-distance passenger and freight work. A total of 899 passed to Deutsche Reichsbahn-Gesellschaft (DRG; German State Railways – the name used between 1924 and 1937), being numbered 74.400-543/545-1300. Nos 74.1301-10 were taken over from the Saarbahn whilst Nos 74.1311-21 came from the Lübeck-Büchener Eisenbahn in 1938. Here No 74.409 is seen approaching Trier in late 1959. The last of the type in operation in West Germany were withdrawn in 1968.

Les Folkard/Online Transport Archive

Opposite above: The Maschinenbau-Gesellscaft Karlsruhe constructed seven metre-gauge 'Mallet' 0-4-4-0s in 1918 for use by the military. Two of them were passed to the Eisenbahn Haspe-Voerde-Breckerfeld (HVB; Haspe-Voerde-Breckerfeld Railway) after the war. In 1928, after the electrification of the HVB, one of the duo was sold to the Süddeutsche Eisenbahn-Gesellschaft (SEG; South German Railway) for use on the Bahnstrecke Zell im Wiesental-Todtnau (Zell in Wiesental to Todtnau Railway), where it became No 105. The 11¾-mile line – which was eventually to form part of the Mittebadische Eisenbahn Gesellschaft (MEG; Mid-Baden Railway) on 1 January 1953 following the expiry of the original company's concession – opened throughout on 7 July 1889 and, on 10 August 1960, No 105 is seen at Zell im Wiesental shunting a transfer wagon carrying a standard gauge wagon. Passenger services over the line were withdrawn on 25 September 1960 and freight traffic ceased on 24 September 1967. Following closure, No 105 was preserved and is now based on the Blonay-Chamby museum line in Switzerland.

Charles Firminger/Bob Bridger Collection/Online Transport Archive

Right: The Zabergäubahn (Zabergäu Railway) was a 750mm branch that linked Leonbronn to the main line at Lauffen am Neckar in Baden-Württemberg. The line was opened in two stages: to Güglingen on 28 August 1896 and thence to Leonbronn on 18 October 1901. The line was converted to standard gauge between 3 May 1964 and 25 July 1965 but was finally closed to passenger traffic in July 1986. No 99.672, seen outside the shed at Güglingen in August 1961, was one of 47 locomotives delivered to the Deutsche Reichsbahn-Gesellschaft (DRG; German State Railways) between 1923 and 1927. The locomotive was built Henschel und Sohn in 1923 and was withdrawn as a result of the line being converted to standard gauge. Sister locomotive No 99.716 is preserved.
Phil Tatt/Online Transport Archive

Above: Class 39 2-8-2 No 39.079 – one of a batch of 12 built by Krupp during 1924 – was one of 260 of the type constructed between 1922 and 1927 and is seen here in March 1962 at Stuttgart Hauptbahnhof. The origins of the class lay with the Preußische Staatseisen-bahnen; designed in 1919 by Borsig-Werke under the supervision of chief engineer August Meister, the first of the proposed Class P10 were not completed until after the railway was merged into the new Deutsche Reichseisenbahnen in 1920 as a result of the shortage of materials after the end of World War. The three-cylinder locomotives were the most powerful of the various Länderbahn classes inherited from the various state railways. After World War 2 a number of the class were inherited by PKP (Polish State Railways) and 152 passed to Deutsche Bundesbahn (DB). The last operation in West Germany was in the Stuttgart area, from where the final three examples were withdrawn in 1967. Two of the class – Nos 39.184 and 39.230 – survive in preservation along with five of the East German examples that were rebuilt into Class 22 between 1958 and 1962.
Phil Tatt/Online Transport Archive

Right: As trams pass above, Class 01 01.228 – built by Kassel & Sohn in 1938 – awaits departure from Hamburg Hauptbahnhof in 1963. A total of 231 of this type of two-cylinder 4-6-2 were delivered between 1926 and 1938; the type represented the first of the Einheitsdampflokomotiven (or 'standard steam locomotives'); No 01.228 was one of the last to be completed. A further 10 of the Class 02 four-cylinder compound version, which had been built in 1926 for comparison purposes, were converted to two-cylinder between 1937 and 1942. A total of 165 of the class passed to DB when it was established on 7 September 1949. After 1957 50 of the class – including No 01.228 – were rebuilt with high performance welded boilers and a 'Mischvorvarmer' in the smokebox. The rebuilt locomotives were identifiable as a result of their modified frames. The last '01s' were withdrawn in June 1973; No 01.228, which became No 001.228-6 in early 1968, was withdrawn in March 1968.
Charles Firminger/Bob Bridger Collection/Online Transport Archive

Above: The Bottwarbahn (Bottwar Railway) was a 750mm line that linked Marbach with Heilbronn. At some 23 miles in length it was the longest narrow gauge line operated by the Königlich Württembergischen Staats-Eisenbahnen (KWStE; Royal Württemberg State Railways) and opened in stages between 1894 and 1900. Although diesel traction was introduced to the line after the war, competition saw the line's economics deteriorate during the early 1960s and passenger traffic was withdrawn on 24 September 1966; freight traffic over the remaining narrow gauge section ceased 30 September 1968. During the summer of 1965

No 99.650 is seen at Oberstenfeld with a mixed train towards Marbach. The locomotive was one of 15 0-10-0s built towards the end of World War 1 by Henschel und Sohn. Two of the type – Nos 99.650 and 99.651 – were used between 1928 and 1964 on the line between Biberach and Ochsenhausen before being transferred to the Bottwarbahn. Following the closure of the line between Heilbronn and Marbach, No 99.650 was scrapped but sister No 99.651 survives in preservation and is currently based on the Öchsle museum railway.
Phil Tatt/Online Transport Archive

Above: Pictured awaiting from the terminus at Westerland (Sylt) is Class 03 4-6-2 No 03.066. The '03' was first introduced in 1930 as a lighter version of the earlier Class 01. Up to No 03.123, the maximum axle-load was 17 tonnes; for subsequent locomotives this was increased to 18 tonnes. A total of 298 were completed by the time that construction ceased in 1938. No 03.066 was built by Henschel und Sohn in 1932 and was to survive until withdrawal in July 1967. Only 45 of the type remained operational in 1968 – including six based in Bremen, one at Husum and 13 at Hamburg-Altona – with the last DB examples being withdrawn four years later. The branch line to Westerland, on the holiday island of Sylt, was opened on 1 June 1927.
Phil Tatt/Online Transport Archive

Above: In August 1966 Class 23 2-6-2 No 23.076 is seen at Lingen station. The type was introduced in 1950 for light express passenger services and, as designed, included the most up-to-date features of German locomotive practice, including welded frames and boilers. A total of 105 were constructed by four manufacturers – Henschel & Sohn (29), Arnold Jung Lokomotivfabrik (51), Krupp (21) and Maschinenfabrik Esslingen (4) – by 1959 when construction ceased. No 23.105 was the last steam locomotive constructed for use on DB. No 23.076 was one of the batch completed by Arnold Jung Lokomotivfabrik and was new in 1956. Withdrawn in October 1975 having been renumbered 023.076-3 in 1968, the locomotive was preserved two years later when it was sold to the Dutch-based Veluwsche Stoomtrein-Matschappij (VSM). Seven other examples of the type also survive.
Phil Tatt/Online Transport Archive

Above: Constructed by Krupp in 1957, the two locomotives of Class 10 were designed to be the forerunners of a type to replace older Pacific classes but, as a result of their high axle load (which restricted them to specific routes) and other problems, no further examples of the type were completed. Utilising a number of design initiatives – such as a fully-welded boiler and semi-streamlining – the type was intended to see reduced operational and maintenance costs. When new No 10.001 was partially oil-fired but, as seen here in 1966, had been converted to fully oil-firing (as No 10.002 had been from new). Initially allocated to Bebra, the duo were transferred to Kassel – where No 10.001 is pictured on 6 November 1966 – in 1962, seeing service on express services to Gießen until March 1967. No 10.002 was withdrawn following a broken side rod in January 1967 (and scrapped five years later); No 10.001 then operated on services to and from Münster until withdrawal in January 1968. No 10.001 was subsequently preserved.

Charles Firminger/Bob Bridger Collection/Online Transport Archive

Above: On 8 November Class 44 three-cylinder 2-10-0 No 44.1366 is seen at Bullay with a freight. Introduced in 1926, was one of the class of Einheitsdampflokomotiven ('standard steam locomotives') introduced by the DRG after 1925. A total of 1,989 of the type were built before construction ceased in 1949 including a number of the austerity model – designated Class 44ÜK (or Übergangskriegslokomotiven ['provisional war locomotives']) – with 1,242 passing to DB. After the war the class was also to be found in East Germany, Poland, Czechoslovakia, Austria and France. A single examples that passed to SNCB in Belgium was returned to Germany in 1950 before being sent to France two

years later. In the late 1950s 32 of the DB-based locomotives were converted to oil-burning and redesignated as Class 43; the last of these were withdrawn by DB in 1968 whilst the last coal-fired examples were withdrawn in 1977. No 43.1366 was built as one of the Class 44ÜKs, being completed by Krupp in 1942. It was to achieve almost exactly a quarter century of operation before withdrawal in January 1967; it was scrapped early the following year. More than 40 of the type survive in preservation, including a number from the same batch that Krupp supplied in 1942 to No 44.1366.

Charles Firminger/Bob Bridge Collection/Online Transport Archive

Above: One of the most successful designs to emerge as part of the Einheitsdampflokomotiven programme, the Class 50 2-10-0 heavy freight locomotive first emerged in 1939. By the time production ceased in 1948, 3,164 had been built. Of these, 2,159 were to form part of the DB fleet and provided the operator's primary freight locomotive through the 1950s and into the 1960s. Although withdrawals had seen the numbers reduced, some 1,450 remained in service in 1968 when DB undertook its reclassification scheme. On 17 July 1967, No 50.341 is seen in Cologne heading a freight. This locomotive was built by Henschel & Sohn in 1940 and was to be renumbered 050.341-7 in 1968; it was withdrawn in March 1974. The last DB examples were withdrawn from service three years later.
John Worley/Online Transport Archive

Right: On 15 September 1967 a Class 41 2-8-2 runs parallel to Columbuskaji, Bremerhaven, as it departs from the quay northbound. The Class 41 Einheitsdampflokomotiven was developed during the mid-1930s in response to the needs of DRG for a fast locomotive for freight traffic. Designed by Friedrich Wilhelm Eckhardt, the first two prototypes were completed in 1937 and large scale production commenced in October 1938. In all a total of 366 were constructed by numerous manufacturers, including Borsig, Krupp and Orenstein & Koppel between then and June 1941. After the war, DB acquired 216 of the class with DR operating 122. Between 1957 and 1961, 107 of the type were fitted with replacement fully-welded boilers as a result of metal fatigue affecting the originals; 40 of these modified locomotives were equipped for oil-firing and were subsequently designated Class 042.
Alan Murray-Rust/Online Transport Archive

Above: Seen passing over the Billhorner Brückenstraße to the east of Hamburg en route towards Bergedorf in September 1967 is Class 94 0-10-0T No 94.871. Developed from the earlier Preußische Staatseisenbahnen Class T16, the Class T16.1 was first introduced in 1913 primarily for freight traffic and shunting work. By the end of 1924, when production ceased, a total of 1,242 of the type had been built by five different manufacturers.

After World War 2, the type saw service in both East and West Germany, being redesignated as Class 094 by DB in 1970. The last of the DB-allocated examples were withdrawn in 1974; No 94.871, which had been built by BMAG in 1919, was withdrawn on October 1968.
Phil Tatt/Online Transport Archive

Above: Designed by Robert Garbe for the Preußische Staatseisenbahnen, the Class G8.1 0-8-0 was a development of the earlier Class G8 as a 'strengthened standard class' and was first introduced in 1913. With larger boilers, the new class had a higher tractive effort than its predecessor but its higher axle loading meant that its operation was more restricted. Primarily designed for freight traffic, the class was also employed on shunting duties. With more than 5,000 constructed, the class was the single largest built for operation in Germany although almost 700 were converted to 2-8-0s between 1934 and 1941. More than 1,000 of the class were still in operation after the end of World War 2 and, in 1968 (when the class was redesignated as 055), DB still had 50 in service. The last of the West German examples were withdrawn in late December 1972. On 17 March 1968 No 055.345-3 was used on a railtour in conjunction with Class 65 No 65.001 and is seen here at Bailstein receiving attention. Originally No 55.3345 and built by Henschel und Sohn in 1915, the locomotive is preserved – the only example of this once numerous type to survive from DB.

Charles Firminger/Bob Bridger Collection/Online Transport Archive

Above: On 22 June 1968 Class 65 2-8-4T No 65.003 departs from Darmstadt with a suburban service. The type was introduced in 1951, when 13 were constructed by Krauss-Maffei, to replace Classes 78 and 93.5 and were thus allocated to the depots at Darmstadt, Düsseldorf and Letmathe. A further five locomotives – Nos 65.014-18 – were constructed in 1956 by the same manufacturer and equipped for push-pull operation. With limited coal capacity and small water tanks, the range of the type was restricted but, despite early teething problems (they were withdrawn temporarily in 1952 to be strengthened around the base of the dome) and problems with the running gear, the type proved reliable eventually. The first was withdrawn in 1966 and all had been taken out of service by the end of 1972; No 65.003 succumbed after accident damage incurred in early December 1969 being formally withdrawn on 4 March 1970. The last of the class is preserved in The Netherlands.
Les Folkard/Online Transport Archive

Above: Pictured awaiting departure from Emden West on the 3.38pm service to Aussenhafen on 24 August 1968 is Class 82 0-10-0T No 82.025. The first of DB's Neubaudampflokomotiven (newly designed steam locomotives), a total of 41 of the type were constructed between 1950 and 1955. The first 22 were built by Krupp, the next 10 by Henschel and the final nine by Maschinenfabrik Esslingen. No 82.025 was one of those completed by Henschel in 1950. Built primarily for freight and shunting duties, the locomotives were to be found working in the marshalling yards at Bremen and Hamm as well as harbour lines around Emden and Hamburg. In order to improve operation on lines with sharp radius curves – such as those encountered on the harbour lines of Hamburg – the first and last axles were fitted with Beugniot levers to improve flexibility. The last of the class was withdrawn from service in 1972 and was subsequently preserved. *Charles Firminger/Bob Bridger Collection/Online Transport Archive*

Right: On 9 September 1968 Class 38.[10-40] 4-6-0 No 38.2259 is seen arriving at Horb with a service from Rottweil to Stuttgart. Designed by Robert Garbe for the Prussian State Railways and originally Class P8, almost 4,000 of the type were constructed for operation in Germany (3,561) between 1908 and 1923) with a further 65 produced for Poland and 321 for Romania. Following World War 1, a number of the class passed to other European railways as reparations although post-war construction of further locomotives of the class replaced these. The last of the type in service with DB were withdrawn in 1974 and more than a dozen survive in preservation. *Charles Firminger/Bob Bridger Collection/Online Transport Archive*

Above: In September 1968, as work is in hand on improvements to the platform in connection with the extension of the S-bahn network from Bergedorf (introduced the following year), Class 78 4-6-4T No 78.521, built in 1924 by Vulcan-Werke of Hamburg and Stettin, is seen awaiting departure from Aumühle with a service towards Bergedorf. By this date the locomotive was coming to the end of its career; it was stored later the same month and formally withdrawn three months later. The class represented the last type of tank locomotive built for Preußische Staatseisenbahnen with the first of the 'T18s' being delivered in 1912. By the time production ceased in 1927 a total of 534 had been completed. Of these DB took over 434 and DR 53; the last examples in West Germany were withdrawn on 31 December 1974.
John Worley/Online Transport Archive

Above: On 8 August 1960 Class 298 0-6-2T No 298.56 is prepared at Krimml prior to working the 3.58pm service to Zell am Zee on the 760mm Pinzgaubahn (Pinzgau Railway). The line, which extends to just over 33 miles in length, was originally opened on 3 January 1898. Initially its primary traffic was timber but its proximity to the Krimml Falls – Austria's largest waterfall system – resulted in the growth of tourist traffic. No 298.56 was originally built by Floridsdorf 1900 for the NOLB as No 2; renumbered U.6 in 1906 and BBÖ No U.56 in 1922, following the Anschluss of 1938 it became Deutsche Reichsbahn (DRB) No 99.7822; it retained this number until it received its final number in 1953. Withdrawn in 1982, it was subsequently preserved and is now based on the Stainzerbahn (Stainz Railway) based at Stainz.
Charles Firminger/Bob Bridger Collection/Online Transport Archive

Above: After 1918 the Austrian section of the Kaiserlich-königliche Österreichische Staatsbahnen (KKStB; Royal Austrian State Railways) became the Deutschösterreichische Staatsbahnen (DÖStB) and which was renamed the Österreichische Staatsbahnen (ÖStB; Austrian State Railways) in 1919. It was renamed Bundesbahn Österreich (BBÖ) in 1923; it was not to become Österreichische Bundesbahnen (ÖBB) until 1947 after a Swiss railway, which had previously used the initials ÖBB changed its name. The 18 Class 97.2s (KKStB/BBÖ Class 69) were 0-6-2Ts built by Lokomotivfabrik Floridsdorf AG between 1890 and 1908 for operation on the Erzbergbahn, a standard gauge line

connecting Leoben with Hieflau. The first section of the line – from Leoben to Vordernberg – was opened on 18 May 1872 but the route – with its central Abt rack section – was not finally completed until the early 1890s. Although the number of working steam locomotives were gradually withdrawn from 1944, the last were not taken out of service until 1978 when the rack system was finally discontinued. No 97.217 – seen here approaching Vordernberg in July 1961 – was one of five of the type eventually fitted with Giesl ejectors; on withdrawal, the locomotive was preserved and is now displayed at Vordernberg.
Phil Tatt/Online Transport Archive

Right: In July 1961 ÖBB Class 77 4-6-2T No 77.17 is seen at Gleisdorf, to the south of Graz. This was one of 85 locomotives constructed in four batches between 1913 and 1928; the first were constructed for the Südbahn (Southern Railway) as Class 629. Passing to the BBÖ, the type was redesignated as Class 77 following the Anschluss of 1938. Further locomotives were constructed for ČSD (Czechoslovak State Railways) during the 1920s and 1930s – as Class 354 – and, after World War 2, a number of the BBÖ examples were to pass to both ČSD and JŽ (Yugoslavian State Railways). Four ÖBB examples survive in preservation, as does one those operated by JŽ. In addition, three of those constructed for ČSD are also preserved.
Phil Tatt/Online Transport Archive

Right: Also recorded at Gleisdorf in July 1961 is Graz-Koflacher Bahn (GKB; Graz to Koflach Railway) 4-4-0 No 406. This locomotive was originally constructed for the Südbahn by Wiener Neustadt in 1896 as No 406 before it became BBÖ No 503.14. Withdrawn in 1927, it was sold to the GKB where it reverted to its original number. By the date of this photograph, the locomotive was approaching the end of its long career; it was withdrawn the following year and subsequently preserved. It is currently displayed at the Slovenian Railway Museum in Ljubljana.
Phil Tatt/Online Transport Archive

Right: At the start of the 20th century the region of north-east Styria was opened up by the construction of the Feistritztalbahn (the line from Weiz to Birkfeld that was subsequently extended to Ratten). Extending for some 26 miles, the 760mm line was designed to help exploit the area's rich timber resources as well as the coal deposits around Ratten. The initial section to Birkfeld was opened in December 1911 with the Ratten section being finally completed in 1930. The Ratten line was never to carry passenger services and was to decline following the closure of the mine in 1960; it was finally to close in February 1971.

Regular passenger services over the original 15-mile section to Birkfeld ceased on 2 June 1973 but, two years prior to that, a steam operated tourist service had been introduced alongside the surviving freight traffic. In July 1961 0-6-2T No U.7 is pictured at one of the intermediate stations – Anger – with a passenger service. This was one of 54 similar narrow-gauge locomotives constructed between 1894 and 1922; of these 43 were built for the KKStB with the remainder destined for three other railways. The type was designated Class 298 by ÖBB. No U.7 was built by Krauss at its Linz factory in 1899; since 1921 the locomotive has been based on the Steiermärkische Landesbahn (StLB; Styrian State Railways), where it remains albeit out of action at time of writing.
Phil Tatt/Online Transport Archive

Above: The Class 93 (BBÖ Class 378) 2-8-2T was designed by Alexander Lerner primarily for use on secondary routes, for which, with its light axle loading, it was ideally suited. One of two standardised designs introduced in 1927 (the other being the Class 392 0-8-0T), a total of 167 were completed between then and 1931 for the BBÖ; a further 26 were completed for other railways during World War 2. Of the 167 operated by the BBÖ, 11 were destroyed during the war and 28 passed to Yugoslavia, leaving 128 to be operated post-war by the ÖBB. The last was withdrawn in 1982. Here No 93.1427 – originally BBÖ No 378.127 – can be seen shunting at Gmund during the spring of 1964.
Harry Luff/Online Transport Archive

Right: On 21 May 1964 Class 52 No 52.3512 awaits its next duty at Graz Hbf shed in the company of diesel No 2050.16. Based upon the pre-war DR Class 50, more than 6,700 of the Class 52 Kriegslokomotiven ('War Locomotives') were built between 1942 and the end of that decade to the design of Richard Felix Paul Wagner. Designed primarily for use on the Eastern Front, examples were to pass to the railway operators of many east European railways in the post-war years. A total of 13 manufacturers constructed the type with No 52.3512 being completed at the Munich-based Krauss-Maffei in 1943. The locomotive survived until 1973; the last of the class in operation on ÖBB were withdrawn in 1986.
Charles Firminger/Bob Bridger Collection/Online Transport Archive

Right: The 25-mile GKB, which links Graz with Koflacher, was originally proposed in the early 1850s but it was not until later in the decade that work on its construction commenced. It was opened for coal traffic in June 1859 with passenger services commencing on 3 April 1860. The line – which is still operational – became a popular haunt for enthusiasts in the late 1970s as it was one of the last railways in the country to operate steam. One of the railway's fleet of locomotives was this 2-6-2T No 301.109 pictured on 21 May 1964. This had originally been KKStB No 13009 when built by Lokomotivfabrik der StEG in 1900, being renumbered 30.109 five years later. It was to pass to the GKB in 1932 and is now preserved. A total of 113 of the design were built for the KKStB between 1895 and 1901, with the survivors eventually becoming ÖBB Class 90. The last ÖBB examples were withdrawn in 1957 and two others – Nos 30.33 and 30.114 – survive in preservation.
Charles Firminger/Bob Bridger Collection/Online Transport Archive

Above: On 21 May 1964 Class 56 2-8-0 No 56.3268 is pictured departing from Graz Koflacherbahnhof with the 5.14pm service to Wies-Eibiswald. Designed by Karl Golsdorf, the first of the class was completed in 1897 for the KKStB and originally designated Class 170. Production continued through until 1918 by which date almost 780 had been completed. After the dissolution of the Austro-Hungarian Empire, the type was to see service in Czechoslovakia, Hungary and Yugoslavia, as well as Austria itself.

The Austrian locomotives were to remain Class 170 under the BBÖ before being reclassified following the Anschluss. No 56.3268 was originally No 170.679 and was new in 1919. Withdrawn finally, in 1970, it was one of the last examples operational in Austria. Although no ÖBB-operated locomotives of the type survive, one operated by the GKB (No 56.3115) does as do seven examples in Eastern Europe.
Charles Firminger/Bob Bridger Collection/Online Transport Archive

Right: The second standard design introduced for the BBÖ in 1927 was the Class 478 (ÖBB Class 392) 0-8-0T, of which 50 were constructed primarily for heavy shunting work. The two standard designs incorporated identical superheated boilers, motion, axleboxes, tanks and other details. Here No 392.2532 – formerly BBÖ No 470.32 – is recorded at Bruck an der Mur on 22 May 1964 towards the end of its life. Two of the class survive in preservation.
Charles Firminger/Bob Bridger Collection/Online Transport Archive

Above: On 22 May 1964 Class 35 two-cylinder 2-6-2 No 35.212 is pictured light engine at Selzthal. First introduced in 1909 by the KKStB as Class 429, the type was designed by Karl Gölsdorf, the then chief design engineer of the railway, primarily for passenger work. A total of 126 compound (Nos 429.100-225) and 197 two-cylinder (429.900-99 and 429.1900-96) locomotives were constructed by three manufacturers by the time production ceased in 1916. Following the break-up of the Austro-Hungarian empire, the class was split, with examples seeing service in Czechoslovakia, Hungary, Italy, Poland, Romania and Yugoslavia as well as Austria itself, where 87 locomotives – 46 compound and 41 two-cylinder – passed to the BBÖ. The locomotives were redesignated as Class 35 in 1938; after the war the surviving compound locomotives were again redesignated, this time as Class 135. No 35.212 was built in 1913 and had originally been KKStB No 429.924; it was to be withdrawn in December 1966. One of the Austrian-based two-cylinder locomotives survives as do two in Eastern Europe (one in the Czech Republic and one in Poland).
Charles Firminger/Bob Bridger Collection/Online Transport Archive

Above: The 760mm gauge Zillertalbahn (ZB; Zillertal Railway) extends for almost 20 miles from the main line station at Jenbach, on the route from Innsbrick to Salzburg, through the valley of the River Ziller to Mayrhofen. The line opened throughout on 31 July 1902 and remains operational, although primarily now operated by diesel traction. The Linz factory of Krauss & Co supplied two 0-6-2T locomotives to the railway in 1900; these were Nos 1 *Raimund* and 2 *Zillertal*. These were followed by a third Krauss-built locomotive – No 3 *Tirol* – in 1902 and it is this locomotive pictured at the junction station of Jenbach in early 1966 with the 10.40am service to Mayrhofen. Both Nos 2 and 3 remain operational with the railway; No 1 is also still extant and in the ownership of the railway but is on display at the Jenbacher Museum.
Harry Luff/Online Transport Archive

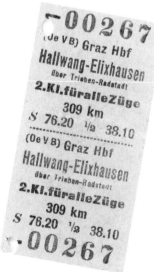

Right: The Steyrtalbahn (Steyr Valley Railway) was a 760mm line that linked Garsten with Klaus. A branch from Pergern via Sierning ran through to Bad Hall. The two routes totalled some 34 miles in length and were opened progressively between 1868 and 1909. Although the branch was closed beyond Sierning in 1933, the remainder and the main line survived intact until the 1960s. The final section to survive, from Garsten to Grünburg, closed in 1982; however, the bulk of the surviving route was to be preserved and reopened in 1985. One of the lines Class 298 0-6-2Ts – No 298.102 – is seen here at Pergern on 9 April 1966. This had originally been Steyrtalbahn No 2 *Sierning* and was new in 1888. Withdrawn in 1973, the locomotive was preserved and is now based on the heritage line.
Charles Firminger/Bob Bridger Collection/Online Transport Archive

Left: On 12 April 1966 Class 770 2-4-0T No 770.95 is pictured arriving at Neustift with the 2.20pm service from Kiernberg-Gaming. The Class 770 originated with 97 locomotives produced for Königlich Bayerische Staats-Eisenbahnen (Royal Bavarian State Railways) by Krauss between 1909 and 1915 and designated Class Pt2/3. Becoming Deutsche Reichsbahn-Gesellschaft (DRG; German State Railways) Class 70, 89 were to pass to Deutsche Bundesbahn (DB; German Federal Railway) after World War 2 but four – Nos 770.86/92/95/96 – remained in Austria and were taken over by ÖBB. The last – No 770.86 – was withdrawn in January 1967 and preserved.
Charles Firminger/Bob Bridger Collection/Online Transport Archive

Right: For operation over the 12-mile rack section of the Erzbergbahn (Erzberg Railway) two 2-12-Ts were constructed by Florisdorf in 1942. Originally DRB Class 97.4, the duo were classified Class 297 by ÖBB. On 14 April 1966 No 297.401 is seen awaiting its next duty at Vordenberg shed. By this date the locomotive was approaching the end of its life; it was to be withdrawn in 1968 and was subsequently preserved. *Charles Firminger/Bob Bridger Collection/Online Transport Archive*

Above: Introduced by the Deutsche Reichsbahn-Gesellschaft (DRG) in 1928, a total of 775 Class 86 2-8-2T Einheitsdampf-lokomotiven (standard steam locomotives) were constructed between then and 1943 when production ceased; those built after 1942 were simplified and known as Übergangskriegs-lokomotiven (provisional war locomotives). The most obvious change was the loss of the second side window in the cabs. After the war, whilst the majority of the class remained operational in West Germany (385) and East Germany (175), other examples passed to ÖBB (29) as well as to the Soviet Union, Poland and Czechoslovakia. Although ÖBB started to withdraw the type as early as 1945, it was not until 1972 that the last was taken out of service. On 13 June 1968 No 86.789 is seen at Eisenerz with the 7.18am service from Leoben to Hieflau. The Eisenerz area was one of the centres of the Austrian iron and steel trade; the Erzberg (Ore Mountain) was one of the richest sources of iron ore in the country and was connected to Eisenerz via the Erzbergbahn. Eizenerz possessed some 25 furnaces producing iron and steel and some of the infrastructure associated with the iron and steel trade can be seen in the background.

Charles Firminger/Bob Bridger Collection/Online Transport Archive

Above: The 2ft 7½in (800mm) Brienz Rothorn Bahn (BRB) is a rack railway, using the Abt double lamella system, that extends for 4¾ miles from Brienz to the summit of the Brienzer Rothorn (7,362ft above sea level). The maximum gradient for the line is 1 in 4 and the line is the fourth highest in Switzerland. Originally opened on 17 June 1892, operation of the line was suspended on 1 August 1914 as a result of World War 1 but was not to reopen until 13 June 1931; although not operational, maintenance of the stock and route ensured that both were in good order when the line did reopen. Unlike most other Swiss lines, the BRB has never been electrified and motive power has always provided by the line's steam locomotives (although the line has also acquired diesel locomotives since 1973). Pictured descending towards Brienz in July 1963 with the Brienzersee in the background is 0-4-2T No 7; this was the last of eight steam locomotives delivered to the line by the Winterthur-based Schweizerische Lokomotiv- und Maschinenfabrik (SLM) between 1891 and 1936. Like the locomotives on a number of steeply graded rack lines, the boilers on the BRB fleet are set at an angle to the frames to ensure adequate water coverage in the boiler when on the steep gradients.

Phil Tatt/Online Transport Archive

Above: On 27 August 1964 BRB No 7 is pictured again, this time
as the SLM-built locomotive of 1936 receives attention at Planalp,
a station situated approximately midway up the line.
John McCann/Online Transport Archive

21.06.65
Valable **2** jours

Lausanne
Bulle
Palézieux-Châtel-St-Denis

1. Cl. ⑩ Fr 11.—

Lausanne - Bulle
via Palézieux
■ Fr 11.—

00932

Above: For the opening of the first section of the future Rhätische Bahn (RhB; Rhaetian Railway) from Landquart to Klosters in 1889 and thence to Davos the following year, Schweizerische Lokomotiv- und Maschinenfabrik (SLM) supplied five metre-gauge Class G3/4 2-6-0Ts. As the railway was extended further locomotives to the same design were again supplied by SLM in 1896 – Nos 6-8 – and between 1901 and 1908 – Nos 9-16. However, the electrification of the railway between 1913 and 1922 rendered many of the line's steam locomotives redundant and, by the end of the 1920s, only three of the type

remained on the RhB – Nos 11, 13 and 14 – for use as shunters and when the power failed. No 13 was scrapped in 1950 but the remaining two soldiered on into the 1970s. No 14 was withdrawn in 1972 and No 11 five yeas later; both were subsequently preserved (as was No 1 which was retained following withdrawal in 1928). Here No 11 – carrying the name *Heidi* after the film in which it appeared during 1952 – is seen at Landquart on 16 June 1966.
Charles Firminger/Bob Bridger Collection/Online Transport Archive

Left: Between 1904 and 1915 the RhB strengthened its locomotive fleet through the purchase of 29 Class G 4/5 2-8-0s Nos 101-29 primarily for operation over the Albulabahn (Albula Railway), which opened in two stages on 1 July 1903 and 10 July 1904. As with the earlier locomotives the 2-8-0s were constructed by SLM but most were destined to have a relatively short career on the RhB as the electrification of the Albulabahn in 1919 rendered them largely redundant. Three were withdrawn in 1920 and sold to the Ferrocarril de La Robla (Robbia Railway) in Spain. A further two were sold to the Estrada de Ferro Maricá in Brazil in 1924 and 18 were sold to the Royal State Railways of Siam in 1926 or 1927. This left six still operational after World War 2 but four of these were withdrawn between 1949 and 1952 and again sold to the Ferrocarril de La Robla. The two remaining locomotives – Nos 107 and 108 (both of which were built in 1906) – were retained on the RhB and used on special services. On 17 June 1966 No 107 is pictured on a special at Filisur.
Charles Firminger/Bob Bridger Collection/Online Transport Archive

Right: On 6 June 1968 Viztnau-Rigi Bahn (VRB; Vitznau to Rigi Railway) No 17 stands at the terminus at Vitznau prior to propelling a train up the 4¼-mile line to Rigi Kulm. Over the distance, the train will ascend some 1,440 yards. Engineered by Niklaus Riggenbach, Ferdinand Adolf and Olivier Zscokke, the standard gauge VRB, known originally as the Rigibahn, opened from Vitznau to Rigi Staffelhöhe on 21 May 1871; it was extended to Rigi Kulm on 27 June 1873. The Riggenbach rack railway was electrified in 1937 but two of the line's steam locomotives – Nos 16 and 17 (the last to be built for the railway) – were retained and used to work special services up the mountain. No 17 was constructed by SLM in 1925; No 16 came from the same manufacturer two years earlier.
Charles Firminger/Bob Bridger Collection/Online Transport Archive

Left: On 6 May 1964 four-cylinder 2-10-0 No 19.39 of Bulgarian State Railways (BDZ) is recorded outside the shed at Septemvri. The four-cylinder mixed traffic locomotive was one of 70 – originally numbered 901-70 – that were constructed by Hanomag between 1913 and 1918. Equipped with superheaters the class was designed for heavy services over steeply graded lines. Latterly, the class was concentrated in the central and eastern areas of the country but, by the late 1960s, they were largely relegated to secondary traffic. Two of the type – Nos 19.25 and 19.62 – survive.
Charles Firminger/Bob Bridger Collection/Online Transport Archive

Above: Bulgaria did not possess a significant number of narrow gauge lines – unlike other countries in the Balkans – but there were two 760mm lines, one of which linked Cerven Briag with Orjahovo. This line was re-equipped in the immediate post-World War 2 era with 20 2-10-2s Nos 601[76]-620[76]. The first 10 were built in East Germany whilst the next 10 came from the Polish manufacturer Chrzanów. Here, on 7 May 1964, examples from both manufacturers – Nos 612[76] leading and 609[76] trailing – are seen taking water at Avramov Kolbe (on the second of the 760mm lines from Septemvri to Dobrinishete to which a number had been transferred). The 65-mile long line from Cerven Briag with Orjahovo was finally to close in 2002. Five of the type survive, including three – Nos 609[76]-611[76] – on the surviving 760mm line from Septemvri to Dobrinishete.
Charles Firminger/Bob Bridger Collection/Online Transport Archive

Above: Pictured at Prague (Vršovice) on 4 August 1960 is Class 477 4-8-4T No 477.060. In the post-war years, Československé státní dráhy (ČSD; Czechoslovak State Railways) constructed a total of 60 4-8-4T locomotives for passenger work based on the sole Class 475.0. The first 38, which were first introduced in 1951, were designated Class 476.1; these were fitted with mechanical stokers and, as such represented the only entire class so equipped worldwide. The design of the class, however, was not wholly successful as it led to overloading on the trailing bogie; as a result, the final 22 locomotives, introduced in 1955, were modified and these became No 477.039-60. Gradually the older Class 476.1s were modified to become Class 477, being renumbered 477.001-38 although some were noted having been renumbered but not modified. The last of the type were withdrawn from service in 1980 but three of the type – two in the Czech Republic and one in Slovakia – survive in preservation.
Charles Firminger/Bob Bridger Collection/Online Transport Archive

Above: ČSD was first established in 1918 following the collapse of the Austro-Hungarian empire after the end of World War 1. ČSD class numbers were based on three digits: the first gave the number of coupled axles; the second with three added and multiplied by 10 gave the maximum speed in km/h; the third, added to 10, gave the axle loading. Thus Class 475 was a 4-8-2 with a maximum permitted speed of 100km/h and an axle loading

of 15 tonnes. Here No 475.1143 is seen approaching Bratislava with a passenger service on 24 May 1965. A total of 147 of the design were constructed by Škoda Works between 1947 and 1950; the last were withdrawn from service in 1980. A total of six – four in the Czech Republic and two in Slovakia – survive. *Les Folkard/Online Transport Archive*

Right: In the late 1920s, ČSD required a number of powerful tank locomotives to operate heavy local and suburban passenger services. The result was the Class 446.0 (later 456.0 as a result of an increased maximum speed) 2-8-4T, which was based on the earlier Class 455.1 2-8-0. A total of 27 were constructed between 1928 and 1932. Here, No 456.015 is seen at Košice on 26 May 1965. *Les Folkard/Online Transport Archive*

Above: Recorded at Zilina on 26 May 1965 is Class 423 2-8-2T No 434.034; this was one of 13 locomotives supplied by Českomoravská Kolben in 1925. This was one of the 'Standard' classes introduced by ČSD and first entered service in 1922. Designed with light axle loadings for use on branch lines. The first and third batches of 10 were built as non-superheated whilst the second batch of 10 – Nos 423.011-20 – were completed in superheated form for comparison and, from No 423.031 onwards all were built superheated. Production of the type continued through until 1946, by which date 171 had been completed; a further 60 locomotives, with a slightly modified boiler were also built post-war. These were to be designated Class 433.0. The last of the Class 423s were withdrawn from service in 1980 although a number were retained as stationary boilers for a period after withdrawal. Five survive in preservation.
Les Folkard/Online Transport Archive

Above: In 1918 ČSD acquired 306 Class 170 2-8-0 locomotives from the KKStB and between then and 1921 a further 71 were constructed locally. A total of 368 compound locomotives were designated as Class 434.0 but the high cost of maintenance and operation of the type led, in 1924, to the start of a programme to convert the type to superheat with simple expansion utilising new piston-valve cylinders. The conversion programme was relatively slow initially, with work being undertaken at Skoda but from 1930 work accelerated with the result that, by 1938, a total of 266 had been converted. During the war a further 67 were rebuilt and by 1951, when the last work was completed, a total of 345 had been rebuilt. In later years 127 of the class were fitted with Giesl ejectors. Withdrawal of the type commenced before 1970 but it was not until 1980, with the withdrawal of Nos 434.2243/315/327, that the last of the type were taken out of service. A number of the class – including No 434.2186 that remains operational with ČSD – have survived. In this view, No 434.202 – one of the earliest to be rebuilt in 1924 – is seen outside Tesnov shed in Prague on 31 May 1965.

Les Folkard/Online Transport Archive

Above: In 1922 ČSD took over the Buštěhradská dráha (BD; Buschtěhrad Railway), which operated a network of lines linking north-west Bohemia with Prague. A total of some 250 locomotives were taken over at the same time; this included 96 outside-framed 0-6-0s – Nos 180-275 – that had been constructed by Wiener Neustädter Lokomotivfabrik between 1887 and 1907. These were to become ČSD Nos 324.301-396. One of the type – No 324.356 – is pictured here in Prague on 31 May 1965. One of the class survives in preservation in the Czech Republic.
Les Folkard/Online Transport Archive

Opposite above: The ČSD Class 524.0 0-10-0s were taken over from the Kaiserlich-Königliche Österreichische Staatsbahnen (KKStB; Royal Austrian State Railways) in 1918. A total of 420 of the superheated class were constructed by a number of manufacturers between 1911 and 1918. Following the dissolution of the Austro-Hungarian empire, the class was largely split between the state railways of Czechoslovakia, Yugoslavia (Class 28), Hungary (Class 520.5), Romania (Class 50) and Poland (Class Tw12). One of the Czech examples – No 524.0268 – is seen here at Benešov on 2 June 1965. None of the Czech examples survive in preservation.
Les Folkard/Online Transport Archive

Opposite below: In 1947 ČSD introduced a class of 40 4-8-2s built by Škoda – the Class 498.0, which was nicknamed 'Albatross' – for use on express passenger services to replace the older Class 387 4-6-2s. During the late 1950s, electrification work – such as on the line from Prague to Česká Třebová (completed in November 1957) – resulted in the type being transferred to other areas, including Děčín. Withdrawal of the type commenced in 1969 and the last was withdrawn in 1976; two of the type have been preserved. Here, No 498.015 is seen receiving attention on 2 June 1965 at Děčín.
Les Folkard/Online Transport Archive

Right: Recorded at Děčín in Czechoslovakia on 2 June 1965 is Deutsche Reichbahn (DR; East German State Railways) Class 58 No 58.1044. Between 1917 and 1921 Preußische Staatseisenbahnen (Prussian State Railways) took delivery of 1,168 Class G12 2-10-0s from a number of manufacturers. Of these, almost 1,150 passed to DR following World War 2 and more than 300 were still in service in 1968; the last were withdrawn in 1976.
Les Folkard/Online Transport Archive

Above: Between 1962 and 1965 the Meiningen locomotive works of Deutsche Reichbahn (DR) rebuilt 35 Class 01 Pacifics; these were to become Nos 01.501-35 and were known as Reko-01 ('Reko' being an abbreviation of 'Rekonstruktionslokomotive' or reconstruction locomotive). By this date the original locomotives were life-expired but were still essential for heavy passenger duties. The work included the provision of a new boiler allied to the cover of the boiler barrel, which was based on the design of the Czech class 477.0 and which gave a much more streamlined appearance. The resulting locomotives were the most powerful express locomotives to see operation in Germany. Although originally coal fired, those converted from 01.519 onwards were oil fired; the latter, however, were amongst the first to be withdrawn as a result of the oil crisis that affected East Germany in the early 1980s. No 01.505 – seen here at Bebra on a cross-border service – had originally been 01.121 and new in 1934; it was converted in 1962. Five of the rebuilt locomotives survive in preservation.
Charles Firminger/Bob Bridger Collection/Online Transport Archive

Above: Between 1897 and 1901 the Nordhausen-Wernigeroder Eisenbahn-Gesellschaft (NWE; Nordhausen-Wernigerode Railway) took delivery of 12 Mallet-type metre-gauge 0-4-4Ts; nine were built by Arnold Jung Lokomotivfabrik with the remaining three being supplied by the Güstrow-based Mecklenburgische Maschinen- und Waggonbau AG. Six of the batch were requisitioned by the military in World War 1 and never returned; the remaining six were rebuilt after the war but one, No 12, was destroyed in an accident in 1927. In the mid-1950s, following the introduction of new locomotives, the surviving five – Nos 99.5901-05 – were transferred from the Nordhausen-Wernigerode to another of the Harz lines, the Selketalbahn (Selke Valley Railway), and it is on this line at Alexisbad, the junction for the branch to Harzegerode, that No 99.5903-2 is seen shunting in August 1970. Two of the five survivors – Nos 99.5904 and 99.5905 – were scrapped in 1990 and 1975 respectively – but the remaining three are still based on the now privatised Harzer Schmalspurbahnen (HSB; Harz Narrow Gauge Railways).
Paul de Beer/Online Transport Archive

Opposite left: The 60cm Waldeisenbahn Muskau (WEM; Muskau Forest Railway) was developed from 1895 into a network extending over some 30 miles in the area between Muskau and Weißwasser in Saxony that was intended to exploit the local forest and mineral resources. After World War 1 the railway's motive power was supplemented by a number of Heeresfeldbahn engines and, by 1939, WEM employed 11 steam locomotives as well as a number of diesels. In 1951 WEM was taken over by DR; at the time of the take-over WEM employed five ex-military locomotives of the 'Brigadelokomotive' design developed after 1901 and which was produced in large numbers from 1905 until the end of the war. One of these – No 99.3313-6 – is seen approaching Bad Muskau on 26 August 1970. All of the steam locomotives were withdrawn in the mid-1970s as the WEM network was rationalised with No 99.3313-6 being preserved in Frankfurt am Main. Although the bulk of the WEM was closed by 1978, a short section was retained for industrial use and, from the late 1980s, this section was preserved with the line being re-extended to Bad Muskau in 1995.
Bernard Harrison/Bob Bridger Collection/Online Transport Archive

Below: After World War 2 DR required additional motive power for operation in the Mittlegebirge, the mountainous area in the south of the country. This resulted in the conversion of 56 locomotives between 1958 and 1962 from Prussian Class G12 2-10-0s into the new Class 58.30 as part of the 'Reconstruction Programme'. The work, which was undertaken at Zwickau Works, included the provision of a new welded cab, newly designed boilers and new welded cylinders. Based primarily in Saxony and Thuringia, one of the class – No 58.3036-0 – is seen at Gera awaiting departure on 27 August 1970. The last of the type were to be withdrawn in February 1981 with two surviving into preservation.
Bernard Harrison/Bob Bridger Collection/Online Transport Archive

Right: On the same day 'Einheitsdampflokomotive' (Standard steam locomotive) No 86.1560-1 – originally No 86.560 – awaits departure from Ave – its home base – with the 12.26pm passenger service to Altenburg. A total of 775 of the Class 86 2-8-2Ts were constructed for the Deutsche Reichsbahn-Gesellschaft (DRG; German State Railways – name used from 1924 to 1937) between 1928 and 1943. Designed primarily for freight traffic, the class – like the Class 58.30s – was predominantly used in the Mittelgebirge and, after the war, 175 of the type passed to DR. Although the East German examples were scheduled for final withdrawal in 1976, a number soldiered on into the next decade and the final examples survived until 1989. A number of the type – including some operated by Austrian railways – survive in preservation.
Bernard Harrison/Bob Bridger Collection/Online Transport Archive

Above: Pictured at Kirchberg on 27 August 1970 is one of the Königlich Sächsische Staatseisenbahnen (KSächsStsEB; Royal Saxon State Railways) Class IVK 750mm 0-4-4-0Ts No 99.1606-5. A total of 96 of this class were constructed between 1892 and 1921, making it the single most numerous class of narrow gauge locomotive in Germany. No 99.1606-5 was built by the Chemnitz-based Sächsische Maschinenfabrik in 1916 and was originally KSächsStsEB No 196; it was to become 99.606 in May 1926. In July 1964 the locomotive underwent complete reconstruction at

the Görlitz works of DR as part of the Rekolokomotiven programme. It was renumbered 99.1606-5 on 1 June 1970. Preserved on withdrawal – one of 22 of the type to survive – the locomotive spent some time on display In Nuremberg before being transferred to the Association for the Promotion of Saxon Narrow Gauge Railways and loaned to the Carlsfeld-based Förderverein Historische Westsächsische Eisenbahnen (Friends of the Historic West Saxon Railways).
Bernard Harrison/Bob Bridger Collection/Online Transport Archive

Above: On 29 August 1970, DR No 95.0044-8 stands in Saalfeld station awaiting departure with the 10.40am service to Sonneberg. A total of 45 of this class of 2-10-2T were constructed between 1922 and 1924 by Borsig-Werke and Hanomag (Hannoversche Maschinenbau AG). Designated as the Prussian Class T20, as development work was initially undertaken by the Prussian State Railways, the type was the most powerful tank engine employed by the DRG. At the end of World War 2, 14 examples passed to DB whilst 31 were operated by Deutsche Reichsbahn (DR) in East Germany. Between 1971 and 1973, 24 of the DR locomotives were converted to oil-firing – being designated Class 95.0 – with those still coal-fired becoming Class 95.1. The last examples in service with DR were withdrawn in 1981; the last of those in West Germany were withdrawn in 1958. Five examples – but not the example recorded here – are preserved.
Bernard Harrison/Bob Bridger Collection/Online Transport Archive

Above: Constructed between 1930 and 1938, the Class 03 4-6-2 Einheitsdampflokomotiven (standard steam locomotives) were designed for express operation over routes suitable for a maximum axle loading of 18 tonnes. A total of 298 were constructed by four manufacturers. Of the locomotives constructed, 86 were to pass into DR ownership and, on 4 July 1971 Borsig-built No 03.203 – by now renumbered 03.2203-2 – is seen at Magdeburg with a service towards Halberstadt. A total of nine Class 03s survive in preservation.
Les Folkard/Online Transport Archive

Right: A second view of a DR Class 03 4-6-2 sees No 03.2028-3 approaching Berlin at Erkner on 8 July 1971. One suspects that this was probably a 'snatched' photograph given that the train was conveying Russian soldiers. The locomotive was built as DRG No 03.028 in 1931 by BLW and it was to survive until withdrawal from Frankfurt (Oder) in early August 1978. It was scrapped later the same year.
Les Folkard/Online Transport Archive

Above: The 750mm Lößnitzgrundbahn (Lössnitz Valley Railway) links Radebeul, to the north-west of Dresden on the main line to Meissen, with Radeburg, a distance of 10¼ miles. Opened by the KSächsStsEB on 16 September 1884, the line saw significant passenger traffic for local residents taking excursions as well as considerable freight traffic, notably coal to the power station at Lößnitzgrund. Surviving the two World Wars, the line achieved its peak passenger traffic in the mid-1950s before a slow and inexorable decline saw it threatened with closure. However, the growth in the tourist industry led to the line being preserved as a 'technical monument' in 1975 and it remains operational. On

11 July 1971 one of the line's 2-10-2Ts, No 99.1786-5, is seen ith a service from Radebeul to Radeburg crossing the electric tramway at Weißer Roß. The DR Class 9.[77-79] were constructed in two batches: Nos 99.771-86 between 1952 and 1954 with Nos 99.787-84 following in 1956. No 99.1786-5 was completed in 1954 as 99.786, being renumbered in June 1970. In 1992 it was again renumbered, this time to 099.750-2 but reverted to its 1970 number in 2007. It is one of a number of the class to be preserved, albeit not currently based on the Lößnitzgrundbahn although five sister locomotives are.

Les Folkard/Online Transport Archive

Above: On 5 September 1964 0-6-0 No 326.477 shunts coaching stock at Debrecen, Hungary's second largest city, which is situated on the Northern Great Plain. The city was first connected to the railway network with the opening of the Tiszavidéki Vasút (Tisza District Railway) from Szolnok – a distance of 75½ miles – on 25 November 1857. The line was extended a further 85 miles to Miskolc via Nyíregyháza on 24 May 1859. The line was nationalised in 1880. No 326.477 was one of the last of a class of 497 0-6-0s constructed between 1882 and 1897.
Les Folkard/Online Transport Archive

Left: Recorded at Balatonfüred on 25 June 1969 is Magyar Államvasutak (MÁV; Hungarian State Railways) No 324.948. The '324' class 2-6-2 was first introduced for mixed traffic in 1909 with 855 being constructed between then and 1921. No 324.948 was one of a batch of 100 delivered during 1916 and 1917. The type was initially designed as a two-cylinder compound but was more successful as a two-cylinder simple design, with 89 of the compound locomotives being converted to simple between 1941 and 1950. As well as seeing service in Hungary, the locomotives also operated after 1924 in Czechoslovakia, Romania, Yugoslavia and Italy. Four of the type have been preserved in Hungary.
Geoffrey Tribe/Online Transport Archive

Above: A total of 510 Class 422 2-8-0s were acquired by MÁV after the end of World War 2. These were ex-US Army Transportation Corps Class S160s and had been built between 1943 and 1945 by a variety of US-based manufacturers. The cost – some $5,100,000 – was funded out of a $150m loan from the US government designed to help post-war reconstruction. The first of the locomotives were received in May 1947 and by January 1948 more than 400 had been prepared for service. Of the 510, 482 actually operated in Hungary with the remaining 28, being in poor condition, being used for spare parts. Prior to operation in Hungary, the locomotives underwent some modification work; this included raising the cab height, increasing the height of the chimneys and replacing the steam engine brake with an air brake. Withdrawal of the type commenced in the mid-1960s and only six remained operational in 1980; all were withdrawn by 1983. Three of the type are preserved in Hungary with a further two in Britain. Here an unidentified member of the class is seen passing over Vágóhíd Utca, south of the centre of Budapest on the east side of the Danube, with a northbound freight on 2 July 1969.
Geoffrey Tribe/Online Transport Archive

Above: The Győr-Sopron-Ebenfurti Vasút (GySEV; the Győr, Sopron & Eberfurth Railway) initially opened between Győr and Sopron – where the railway is based – on 2 January 1876 and was extended to Ebenfurth on 28 October 1879. Following the separation of Austria and Hungary after World War 1, ownership of the line, which crossed the new border, was spilt between the two new countries. In addition to numerous second-hand locomotives operated, the line operated four MÁV Class 375 2-6-2Ts, three of which were acquired new (in 1914, 1916 and 1925) whilst a fourth was acquired second-hand from MÁV in 1953. One of this quartet – No 123 – is seen at Sopron station on 27 September 1969.
Les Folkard/Online Transport Archive

Opposite above: Recorded at Szombathely on 27 September 1969 is No 275.137 as passengers board the train; this was one of 175 2-4-2Ts constructed for use on MÁV between 1928 and 1939. Only two types of tank locomotive were introduced on to MÁV between the two World Wars: this class and the four examples of Class 242 4-4-4s. Originally designated Class 22, the type was subsequently redesignated Class 275. Nine of the type are preserved in the country. Szombathely, situated to the west of the country, is a close to the border with Austria and is a significant railway junction on the main line from Győr to Szentgotthárd.
Les Folkard/Online Transport Archive

Opposite below: Three days later – on 30 September 1969 and further to the south – beyond Lake Balaton – No 326.340 is seen shunting at Kisberény. MÁV acquired 497 of this type of 0-6-0 between 1882 and 1887; the class was a development of the earlier Class 335, which was introduced in 1869, with the only significant difference being an increase in boiler pressure from 121psi to 142. Examples of Class 326 were also manufactured for a number of the non-MÁV lines – such as GySEV – and for operation in Serbia. Although used historically on a variety of traffic – including express passenger turns – in later years the type was more restricted, often on duties such as this, but were generally well turned out with burnished wheel rims. The last examples of the type were still operational in the early 1970s.
Les Folkard/Online Transport Archive

Right: Based on the successful pre-war Class Pt31 2-8-2, the 'Pt47' class of Polski Koleje Państwowe (PKP; Polish State Railways) was first introduced in 1948 and, between then and 1951, a total of 180 were constructed by Fablok of Chrzanów and H. Cegielski–Pozna. The type was designed to operate heavy and fast trains on long-distance routes and, being capable of speeds in excess of 60mph, was to be found widely across the country on express trains operating over non-electrified lines. One of the 120 of the type constructed by Fablok – No Pt47-42 – is pictured at Lublin in 1975. Almost 20 of the class are still extant.
Harry Luff/Online Transport Archive

Above: The PKP Class Ok22 4-6-0 was first introduced in 1923 when five locomotives were built by Hannoversche Maschinenbau AG (Hanomag) with domestic production of the type commencing in 1928. A further 185 locomotives were constructed by Fablok between then and 1934. The design, which was the first to be completed in Poland after the country gained its independence after World War 1, incorporated the chassis of a Prussian Class G8 – which operated in Poland as PKP Class Ok1 – allied to a large, high-pitched boiler, wide firebox and large cab. The Polish class

name for tender locomotives was based around a code: the first letter indicated the type of train ('P' for express, 'O' for stopping passenger train and 'T' for freight) whilst the second letter indicated the wheel arrangement (in this case 'k' stood for 4-6-0 but it could indicate an 0-6-4). Here No Ok22-72 is recorded awaiting departure from Choszczno in 1975. Two of the class – Nos Ok22-23 and Ok22-31 – survive in preservation.
Harry Luff/Online Transport Archive

Above: The PKP code for tank engines was based upon the same principle as that for tender locomotives with the addition of a central 'K' between the two other letters. Thus Class TKw2 – of which No TKw2-81 is seen at Pila in 1975 – was primarily a freight locomotive with an 0-10-0T when arrangement. The origins of this class lay with Prussian State Railways, which introduced the T16.1 in 1913. After World War 1, a number of the class were to be used as part of the post-war reparations with a number passing to SNCB in Belgium and to PKP in Poland. After World War 2, the class was to be more widely spread, with examples operational in Austria, Czechoslovakia and Hungary. Following their withdrawal in Poland, two examples remain in preservation – Nos TKw2-57 and TKw2-114.
Harry Luff/Online Transport Archive

Above: In the early 1930s Căile Ferate Române (CFR; Romanian State Railways) sought to increase the power of locomotives employed on express passenger services. Rather then develop its own design, CFR decided to adopt the Austrian Class 214 2-8-4. Although relatively few were constructed for operation in Austria, CFR acquired 79 between 1936 and 1940, including 13 that were built in Austria, which were designated as Class 142. They were widely employed on the principal expresses operated over CFR and here No 142.015 is seen at Sighișoara with an eastbound service in early 1966.
Harry Luff/Online Transport Archive

Above: One of the most common of all CFR steam locomotives was the Class 230 4-6-0 that had its origins in the Prussian State Railways Class P8, which was first introduced in 1908. Initially 75 were acquired, following the enlargement of the country as a result of the Treaty of Versailles, from German manufacturers. A further 18 were transferred to CFR as a result of post-war reparations and an additional 18 were bought from DRG in 1926. In 1930 German manufacturers constructed a further 20 whilst between 1932 and 1939 the newly-established locomotive workshops at Resita and Malaxa supplied more than 230 additional locomotives. The majority of the latter were conventional but in 1936 20 were built with Lenze and 10 with Caprotti valve gear. These were numbered 230.501-30; the highest numbered of the standard locomotives was No 230.338. Used primarily on passenger services throughout the country, here one of the home-built examples – No 230.204 – is pictured shunting empty coaching stock in Bucharest in early 1966. A significant number of the class are still extant but the fate of many of these is likely to be uncertain as they are recorded as 'dumped'.
Harry Luff/Online Transport Archive

Above: Following the Treaty of Versailles, Romania virtually doubled in size and this meant that the country inherited the railways in areas like Transylvania, Bessarabia and Bukovina. Although CFR also inherited some locomotives and rolling stock from the previous operators of these regions – such as MÁV Classes 301 and 601 – there was a need to supplement these with new locomotives. In 1921 the Czech-based Škoda supplied a total 80 Class 130.5 2-6-0s – Nos 130-501-80 – based upon the pre-war '2000' class. The major difference between the new class and its precursor was the use of a larger firebox, which resulted in the moving forward of the boiler. One of the type – No 130.546 – is seen receiving attention outside Bucharest shed in early 1966; by this date withdrawals were reducing the number in service but many were still operational into the 1970s. Two of the type – Nos 130.503 and 130.525 – are preserved and on display.
Harry Luff/Online Transport Archive

Above: Between 1913 and 1926 the Munich-based Maffei designed and built a class of 40 4-6-2s for CFR; numbered 2201-40, the locomotives were the largest locomotives delivered to CFR prior to World War 1. Built as four-cylinder simple locomotives, the design owed much to the contemporary Pacifics being delivered to the Königliche Bayerische Staats-Eisenbahnen (KBayStsB; Royal Bavarian State Railways). The front-end design was unusual, with the four cylinders arranged line abreast under the smokebox. In order to keep the wheelbase down, the bogie was set back, with the cylinders being set at a slight angle to clear it. In later years the cranks driven by the inside motion led to problems that required their replacement. Despite this, the type was a success and the majority lasted in operation until the 1970s. Here No 2238 is seen outside Bucharest in early 1966. None of the type survive.
Harry Luff/Online Transport Archive

Above: Between 1903 and 1923 the Caminhos de Ferro do Estado (CFE) received 19 4-6-0s – Nos 81-99 – built by two German manufacturers: Borsig-Werke and Maschinenfabrik Esslingen. All bar two of these were to pass to Caminhos de Ferro Portugueses (CP; Portuguese Railways), eventually being renumbered 221-37. Here one of the earliest of the class – No 222 (which was built by Borsig-Werke in 1903) – is pictured at Ermesinde station, some 5½ miles to the north-east of Porto, in about 1960, with a freight. Situated on the main line north from Porto towards Braga, Ermesinde became a junction with the opening of the first section of the Linha do Douro – to Penafiel – on 29 July 1875.
Harry Luff/Online Transport Archive

Opposite above: Braga station first opened on 21 May 1875 with the completion of the line south to Nine (on the route to Porto). A total of 28 2-6-4Ts – Nos 070-97 – were constructed for the Companhia dos Caminhos de Ferro de Portugueses by the Schweizerische Lokomotiv- und Maschinenfabrik (SLM), by Henschel und Sohn of Kassel and by Gerais of Lisbon between 1916 and 1944. No 089 – seen here at Braga – was one of those manufactured by Henschel und Sohn, being completed in 1929. Two of the type – Nos 070 and 094 – survive in preservation.
Harry Luff/Online Transport Archive

Opposite below: Pictured awaiting departing from Barreiro on 4 May 1964 is CP 4-6-0 No 354. This was one of a batch of 15 – Nos 351-65 – built by the German manufacturer Henschel und Sohn between 1911 and 1913 for the Companhia dos Caminhos de Ferro de Portugueses. Situated on the south bank of the Tagus, across from central Lisbon, Barreiro was selected to be the terminus of the Caminho de Ferro do Sul, which was to become the Linha do Sul – or southern line – in the early 20th century. Work started on the construction of the line in 1854 and the first section opened three years later. The route, which extended almost 140 miles from Barreiro to Funcheira, was completed throughout in 1861. Although the station illustrated in this view is still extant, it is now devoid of track, having been replaced by another station slightly to the east.
Les Folkard/Online Transport Archive

Left: New in 1924, oil-burning 4-6-2 No 553 – seen outside Barreiro station on 4 May 1964 – was one of 10 four-cylinder compounds – Nos 551-60 – built by Henschel und Sohn for the Sul e Sueste (SS; South and South-East) Division of CP. For many years the type operated the principal expresses south of the Tagus and were easily identifiable with their four domes. The first and third of these were sandboxes, the second housed a top feed whilst the fourth accommodated the regulator. Following withdrawal, No 553 was preserved.
Les Folkard/Online Transport Archive

Above: Between 1861 and 1881 a total of 35 0-6-0s – Nos 101-35 – were supplied by a number of manufacturers including the British-based Sharp Stewart & Co, at the time based in Manchester, and Kitson & Co of Leeds. By 1950, and the final renumbering of CP's locomotive fleet, the class had been reduced by more than half. Pictured shunting at Setil, situated to the north of Lisbon on the line towards Santarem, on 7 May 1964 is the last of the class, No 135, which was to be preserved following withdrawal and is now based at the railway museum at Entroncamento.
Les Folkard/Online Transport Archive

Above: Seen receiving attention on 8 May 1964 at Sernada are, on the left, 2-6-0T No E.102 and, on the right, 2-6-0T No E.95. The former was one of three metre-gauge locomotives supplied to the Campanhia do Caminho do Ferro de Guimarães (CFG; Guimarães Railway Company) by Maschinenfabrik Emil Kessler of Esslingen in Germany in 1907 for the opening of the extension to Fafe. Regarded as amongst the best of the small narrow-gauge locomotives operated, they survived until the end of steam operation in the Porto area in 1976/77. No E.102 was finally scrapped by July 1987; sister locomotive No E.101 is preserved. No E.95 was one of seven supplied to the Companhia de Caminho de Ferro do Vale do Vouga (VV; the Vouga Valley Railway) in 1910 by Orenstein & Koppel and by Decauville. All were taken out of service between 1974 and 1980 although a number survive; No E.95 was sold after withdrawal to a group in Valencia, Spain. *Les Folkard/Online Transport Archive*

Above: Regarded as amongst the most impressive steam locomotives operated by CP, the three compound 4-8-0s – Nos 801-03 – produced by Henschel und Sohn in 1931 were designed to operate the heavily graded main line of Beira Alta, constructed by the Companhia dos Caminhos de Ferro Portugueses da Beira Alta, which links the Spanish border at Vilar Formosa with the Portuguese main line between Lisbon and Porto at Pampilhosa (the Linha do Norte) just to the north of Coimbra. On 8 May 1964 one of the trio – No 802 – stands with a freight in Entroncamento station. Following withdrawal, one of the class – No 801 – was preserved and is on display at Vilar Formosa. The station name simply means 'junction' and the settlement grew up in the mid-19th century as it was the junction between two of Portugal's main lines – the northern (Linha do Norte) and the eastern (Linha do Lesete) – and, as a result, was one of the most important railway towns in the country.
Les Folkard/Online Transport Archive

Left: In 1945 CP took delivery of 22 2-8-2s manufactured by the American Locomotive Co; numbered 851-60, 1751-56 and 2851-56 in 1948, they were renumbered 851-72 in 1950. The locomotives were allocated to four of CP's divisions; oil-fired No 870 – seen here at Vila Nova de Gaia, to the south of Porto, with a southbound freight towards Entroncamento on 9 May 1964 – was one of six, Nos 867-72 originally based on the Caminho de Ferro Minho a Douro. One of the type – No 855 – survives in preservation.
Les Folkard/Online Transport Archive

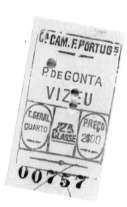

Left: In 1911 the Belgian-based John Cockerill supplied the Caminhos de Ferro do Estado Minho e Douro (MD; the Minho & Douro State Railways) two 2-6-2Ts, Nos 81 and 82, for use on the Porto suburban lines. Following the take-over of the MD by CP in 1927, the locomotives were initially renumbered 02081 and 02082; they were again renumbered in 1950 as 041 and 042. The latter is recorded near Porto Campanhã station on 9 May 1964. Following withdrawal, No 042 was preserved and is now based at Entroncamento.
Les Folkard/Online Transport Archive

Above: On 12 May 1964 CP 2-4-6-0T No E.204 is seen shunting freight stock at Samardã. This locomotive was one of a batch of 11 metre-gauge Mallet tanks supplied by Henschel und Sohn in 1911 to the MD; a further five smaller but similar locomotives were delivered by the same manufacturer in 1923. Samardã was one of the intermediate station on the Corgo line, from Peso de Regua to Chaves; the section of line through the station opened on 12 May 1907. All of the 16 locomotives were withdrawn by the late 1980s; No E.204 succumbed in 1984 but was still extant – but derelict – more than a decade later. A number of the type are officially preserved – including No E.206 in Switzerland – with Nos E.203/207/214/216 in Portugal.
Les Folkard/Online Transport Archive

Left: On 21 May 1967 as a narrow-gauge locomotive is turned on the turntable at Regua, on the main line from Porto to Tua, 4-6-0 No 295 departs from the station with a westbound service towards Porto. The locomotive was one of six – Nos 291-96 – built by Henschel und Sohn in 1913. No 294 is still extant; however, it only survives in a dumped condition at the time of writing at Vila Nova de Gaia. The metre-gauge Linha do Corgo (Corgo Line) ran north from Regua via Vila Real to Chaves – a distance of some 61 miles – and was first opened from Regua to Vila Real with the extension to Chaves finally being completed in 1921. The line was operated by CFE from opening; following the privatisation of CFE in 1928, it was operated by Companhia Nacional (CN; National Company) until taken over by CP in 1947. Steam operation on the Corgo Line continued into the 1970s with limited use with shunters continuing into the next decade. However, the decline in passenger traffic that resulted from road improvements led to the withdrawal of passenger services between Vila Real and Chaves in 1990. On 25 March 2009, following concern over the state of the track, the remaining services from Regua to Vila Real were withdrawn; although there were repairs promised, budgetary constraints have resulted in no work being undertaken.
Charles Firminger/Bob Bridger Collection/Online Transport Archive

Right: Designed primarily for suburban services around Lisbon and Porto, this class of 2-6-4T – Nos 070-097 – was first introduced in 1916 with 15 being supplied by Schweizerische Lokomotiv- und Maschinenfabrik (SLM). A further 12 were built by Henschel und Sohn in 1929 with the final example being constructed in Portugal in 1944, probably using spare parts. Here one of the original Swiss-built examples – No 078 – is pictured at Ermesinde on 23 May 1967. Three of the class – Nos 070, 072 and 094 – survive at Estremoz, Porto and Entroncamento respectively.
Charles Firminger/Bob Bridger Collection/Online Transport Archive

Above: Recorded at Valencia Termino station in 1960 is one of RENFE's Class 462F 4-6-2-2-6-4s No 462.F.0402. This was one of a batch supplied by Euskalduna de Construcción y Reparación de Buques de Bilbao to the Central of Aragon Railway in 1930/31 for use over the mountainous section of the line between Valencia and Calatayud. Following the creation of RENFE on 24 January 1941, the locomotives, which were the heaviest acquired by the new operator, were transferred for use on the heavy express trains from France down the east coast to Valencia via Barcelona, replacing electric traction at Tarragona. Originally coal fired the type was later converted to oil firing. Withdrawn in the late 1960s, one of the class – No 462.F.0401 – was preserved.
Geoffrey Tribe/Online Transport Archive

Left: The 750mm line operated by the Ferrocarril de San Feliu (SFG) extended for a distance of 26 miles from Sant Feliu de Guíxols to Girona in Catalonia. The line opened in 1892 – the first narrow gauge railway in Spain – and was primarily designed to transport freight to the coast at Girona; however, as the tourism developed so it became an increasingly popular means of moving people to and from the seaside. Despite this, by the early 1960s, the line was in decline and it was to close finally in 1969. On 19 June 1962, No 4 is seen at Llagostera, one of the intermediate stations on the line (and source, historically, of harvested cork that was one of the key items of freight transported). No 4 was one of four 0-6-2Ts supplied to the railway for its opening by Lokomotivfabrik Kraus & Cie. No 4 is one of a number of locomotives from the line that survive in preservation locally. The line itself was eventually to be converted into a cycleway and footpath.
Neil Davenport/Online Transport Archive

Left: In all some 200 4-8-2 locomotives operated on RENFE; No 241.2235 was one of a class of 57 introduced in 1944 and built by Barcelona-based La Maquinista Terrestre y Maritima between then and 1952. The type was designed to supplement the existing 4-8-2s employed on the main line inherited from the Compañía de los Ferrocarriles de Madrid a Zaragoza y Alicante (MZA) between Madrid and Alicante via Zaragoza. No 241.2235, which was new in 1951, is seen here awaiting departure from Madrid (Atocha) station in May 1963. The locomotives were originally equipped for coal firing but were later modified to oil burners.
Les Folkard/Online Transport Archive

Above: Until the advent of eight-coupled designs the Ferrocarril de la Compañía del Norte utilised a number of 4-6-0s. In 1904 the Hannoveresche-Maschinenbau-AG (Hanomag) supplied a batch of 30 4-6-0s to the railway. These were to become RENFE Nos 230.2001-30 in 1941 and No 230.2030 is pictured at Castellon in May 1963. The locomotives were employed primarily in their later years on the non-electrified Norte lines. Amongst the routes on which they could be seen the local services in the Valencia area and on the routes from Tarragona to Lérida, Medina del Campo to Salamanca and Alsasua to Pamplona.
Les Folkard/Online Transport Archive

Right: Several hundred 0-6-0s were constructed for use on Spanish railways with many achieving more than a century of operation before withdrawal. During 1863 and 1864 the MZA took delivery of 36 that were built by the French manufacturers Société Usine de Graffenstaden and Schneider et Cie. Built with a shorter wheelbase and smaller tenders than the company's earlier 0-6-0 design, the type was built for use on lightly laid lines with many being employed as shunters in the docks at Málaga and Seville. Here 030.2333 is seen at Seville in October 1965.
Les Folkard/Online Transport Archive

Above: Pictured awaiting departure from Madrid Delicias station in May 1964 is 130.2112. This was one of a batch of 10 locomotives built for the railway that linked Madrid to the Portuguese border via Cáceres that passed to Oeste. All were built by Sächsische Maschinenfabrik Vormals Richard Hartmann of Chemnitz, with the first seven being completed in 1909 and the final three in 1912. Unlike other RENFE 2-6-0 classes, the type was not regularly used on passenger work, being based at Delicias shed and primarily allocated to freight work between Toledo and Villaluenga. Delicias station, designed by Émile Cachelièvre, was opened in March 1880 for the Compañía de los Caminos de Hierro de Ciudad Real a Badajoz; it later passed to the Compañía de los Ferrocarriles de Madrid a Cáceres y Portugal. The station closed in 1969 but now houses the Madrid Railway Museum.
Les Folkard/Online Transport Archive

Left: Inherited by RENFE in 1941 from the Compañía Nacional de los Ferrocarriles del Oeste (Oeste), which had been established in 1928, and originally new to the railway that linked Medina del Campo with Salamanca No 130.2082 was one of a class of six 2-6-0s built between 1910 and 1922 by Kassel-based Henschel und Sohn. The locomotives were transferred from the Oeste area in the 1950s to work on passenger services between Alicante and Murcia, where No 130.2082 is pictured. By the date of the photograph, diesel railcars had appeared on some of the services but there were still four steam workings daily.
Les Folkard/Online Transport Archive

Right: When RENFE was formed in 1941 it inherited a significant number of 4-8-0s from the Norte company of a design constructed between 1909 and 1943 by a variety of manufacturers. In all 436 were built with some being supplied to the Oeste company as well as the Ferrocarril de Alcañiz a la Puebla de Hijar and the Ferrocarril de Murcia a Mula y Caravaca. Amongst the suppliers was Babcock & Wilcox of Bilbao and it was this company that built the last of the type to be constructed. These were RENFE Nos 140.2402-71. One of the batch – No 140.2438 – was subsequently rebuilt with a Franco-Crosti boiler and this locomotive is seen here at Valladolid in May 1960. The modification was not deemed a success and no other Spanish locomotives underwent a similar conversion.
Les Folkard/Online Transport Archive

Right: Although only one of the pre-RENFE companies – Norte – adopted the 2-8-2 design prior to 1941, the newly-nationalised railway company realised that the wheel arrangement was useful and, between 1953 and 1960, acquired 242 of the type from a variety of manufacturers in both Spain and overseas. No 141.2112, seen here on a freight at San Felices on 22 April 1967, was one of the first 25 to be built; these were constructed in Glasgow by the North British Locomotive Co. The type proved adept on a wide range of both passenger and freight duties and were to be seen widely over the RENFE network, including, on occasion, the 'Lusitania Express' – the overnight service that linked Madrid with Lisbon – which was one of the few named express services in Spain. Sister locomotive No 141.2111 is preserved as part of the collection held by the Madrid railway museum.
Les Folkard/Online Transport Archive

Left: Between 1864 and 1865 the Ferrocarril Ciudad Real-Badajoz acquired eight 0-8-0s; these passed in 1872 to the Ferrocarril de Córdoba a Belmez and thus to the Ferrocarriles Andaluces seven years later. In 1891 a further eight locomotives to the same design were supplied by the Belgian-based société de Saint-Léonard and one of this later batch – No 040.2216 – is seen here at Jaen on 22 May 1966. Four of the type were converted into 2-8-0s prior to the creation of RENFE in 1941 whilst the remainder saw service into the late 1960s based around the Puente Genil, Espelúy and Jaen areas.
Les Folkard/Online Transport Archive

Above: Also recorded on 22 May 1966, Class 140.2039 is seen approaching Linares. This was one of a batch of 20 2-8-0s supplied to Ferrocarriles Andaluces in 1927; the first 12 – Nos 140.2029-40 – were built by Babcock & Wilcox and the final eight – No 140-2041-48 – by Euskalduna. The type was used latterly – like many of the ex-Ferrocarriles Andaluces 2-8-0s – on the Almeria to Guadix and Granada lines. There were four similar locomotives supplied by Babcock & Wilcock to Oeste in 1928; these became RENFE Nos 140.2049-52 and were eventually transferred the same area.
Les Folkard/Online Transport Archive

Opposite above: Between 1920 and 1922 the Ferrocarriles Andaluces took delivery of 50 4-8-0s to replace older 2-6-0s on passenger trains. The locomotives were supplied by four manufacturers – Franco-Belge, Borsig, Shwartzkopff and Hanomag – with the first 15 being supplied with six-wheel tenders and the later batches with larger eight-wheeled tenders. On 24 May 1966 one of the last, built by Hanomag in 1922 – No 240.2047 is seen at La Pena with a service from Granada to Bobadilla.
Les Folkard/Online Transport Archive

Opposite below: Recorded at Alcañiz on 26 April 1967 is No 120.2131. The 2-4-0 was the last survivor of a batch of 13 locomotives originally supplied by Esslingen in 1884 to the railway linking Salamanca to the Portuguese border. The locomotives passed to Oeste in 1928 but only two remained in service to pass to RENFE; No 120.2132 was withdrawn in 1955 leaving No 120.2131 as the last survivor of the class in service.
Les Folkard/Online Transport Archive

Above: Only one Spanish railway – the MZA (the Madrid, Zaragoza and Alicante Railway) – acquired any 4-6-4s with 22 being acquired for use on local passenger services primarily in the Madrid area. All were built by Maffei, the first 12 in 1903 and the final 10 in 1911. In later years some of the class moved away from the Madrid area, seeing service in the Murcia, Seville and Vigo areas. On 27 April 1967 No 232.025 – one of the initial batch – is seen about to depart from the now-closed station at Barbastro with a mixed passenger and freight service.
Les Folkard/Online Transport Archive

Right: Whilst Pacific type locomotives were to dominate the main lines in many countries – such as Britain and France – they were relatively uncommon on Spanish metals. One of the Spanish railways that operated a significant number was the MZA, which acquired a batch from the US manufacturer Alco in 1920. A total of 15 were delivered but one of the type – No 912 – was destroyed during the Civil War with the result that only 14 passed to RENFE in 1941. Designed primarily for lightweight express passenger work, the class was eventually to be based in Ayamonte, Huelva and Seville seeing operation on lines such as that from Seville to Carmona (Alta) and to Utrera. It is at Utrera that one of the type – No 231.2022 – is seen taking on water in October 1967.
Les Folkard Online Transport Archive

Right: Spain had a significant number of privately-owned narrow gauge railways; many of these, however, closed in the 1950s and 1960s as a result of increased competition from road traffic. One of the these was the Compañia de los Ferrocarriles Económicos de Villena a Alcoy y Yecla (VAY; Villena to Alcoy and Yecla Railway) to the west of Alicante. Although work on the line's construction commenced in the 1880s it was not until the first decade of the 20th century that the final sections of the line were finally opened. Between 1966 and 1969 the line's locomotive stock was supplemented by the hiring of two 2-6-0Ts produced by La Maquinista Terrestre y Marítima in 1913; these were Nos 5 and 6 and the first of these is pictured at Lorcha on 18 April 1968. By this date the line was approaching the end of its life – it was to be closed in 1969.
Charles Firminger/Bob Bridger Collection/Online Transport Archive

Above: The first section of metre-gauge Piraeus, Athens & Peloponnese Railways (or SPAP) opened between Piraeus, Athens and Elefsis in 1884 and was extended to Corinth in 1885 and thence to Patras two yeas later. A number of branch lines and further extensions followed before the railway was nationalised in 1954; it formally became part of Hellenic State Railways (SEK) in 1962. All metre-gauge operations in Greece were suspended in 2011 as a result of the financial crisis; it's unlikely that they will be resumed. In 1912 Henschel und Sohn supplied five 2-4-0Ts – Nos B.151-55 – to the company and No B.152 is pictured here at work on the dockside at Patria in early 1959. Sister locomotive No B.151 is preserved.
Online Transport Archive

Right: Metre gauge No E.725 – one of five 2-8-0s supplied by Linke-Hofmann-Busch to the SPAP in 1925 – is seen double-heading a freight on 17 June 1961.
Neil Davenport/Online Transport Archive

Left: Five days later, on 22 June 1961, 2-6-0T No 541 is seen departing from Nafplion, the terminus of a branch from Corinth on the SPAP that opened in 1886. The Munich-based Krauss & Co supplied the SPAP with three batches of 2-6-0T – a total of 16 locomotives in all – in three batches with Nos E.540-42 being delivered in 1926. Two of the class – Nos E.540 and E.541 – are preserved and are now on display at Kalamata. *Neil Davenport/Online Transport Archive*

Left: In 1936 Henschel und Sohn supplied the SPAP with a batch of three 2-8-0s – Nos E.726-28 – and one of the trio, No E.727 – which has been fitted for oil firing – is seen in Athens on 22 June 1963. One of the trio, No E.728, is still extant albeit now in a virtually derelict condition. *Neil Davenport/Online Transport Archive*

Above: The four-cylinder Class 685 2-6-2 represented the standard express steam locomotive operated by Ferrovia dello Stato Italiane (FS; Italian State Railways). First introduced in 1912, the type was based on the earlier Class 680 and 106 left-hand drive examples were constructed between then and 1914. A further 165 right-hand drive examples – including No 685.191 seen here in Rome on 7 September 1959 – were completed between 1920 and 1928. Subsequently the class were increased by a further 120 locomotives as a number of the compound Class 680s were rebuilt. With a relatively low axle loading, the class was seen widely across the FS network until electrification started to result in withdrawals. The first to be withdrawn, in the mid-1960s, were some of the rebuilds but all of the class had succumbed by the end of 1975. Four survive in preservation with a fifth retained as a source of spare parts.
Neil Davenport/Online Transport Archive

Above: Between 1911 and 1923 a total of 470 Class 740 2-8-0s entered service with FS. In 1942 five of the type were rebuilt with Franco-Crosti boilers and fitted with streamlined casing; in 1951, with the streamlining removed, these five became Class 743 and a further 88 Class 740s were fitted with Franco-Crosti boilers by 1953. A modified version of the Franco-Crosti rebuild was introduced in 1954. This was Class 741; the major difference between this and Class 743 was the newer version had a single pre-heater under the boiler rather than two placed alongside. In all, a total of 81 locomotives were converted between then and 1960. The type was used primarily in Sicily and in Veneto with the first withdrawals occurring in 1968; the last of the type were withdrawn in the early 1980s. Here No 741.449 is pictured at Vandoles with a freight from Fortezza to San Candido on 29 May 1972. Two of the type are preserved.
Les Folkard/Online Transport Archive

Right: Between 1922 and 1924 FS took delivery of 50 Class 940 2-8-2s primarily for use on railways that served the Appennnine mountains, in particular the important east-to-west line that linked Rome with Pescara via Sulmona. After World War 2, four of the class ended up in Yugoslavia where they were to remain as Jugoslavenske Željeznice (JŽ; Yugoslavian State Railways) Nos 118.001-04. However, three identical locomotives, produced in 1924 for Ferrovie Elettriche Biellesi (FEB; Biellesi Electric Railways) passed into FS and became Nos 940.051-53. From 1968 onwards the class was modified with larger chimney. Here No 940.038 is seen departing from Levice with a service to Trento on 30 May 1972. The '940' class was successful and survived until the end of steam operation on FS, operating on both passenger and freight traffic. A number of the class – but not No 940.038 – survive in preservation.
Les Folkard/Online Transport Archive

Above: Introduced in 1913, the Class 625 2-6-0 was a development of the earlier Class 600 mixed-traffic locomotive. A total of 188 were constructed by two Italian and one German suppliers between then and 1923; these were supplemented between 1929 and 1933 by the conversion of 153 of the older Class 600 locomotives. These were designated Class 625.3. Class 625 was designed to operate both passenger and freight traffic. In the 1950s 25 of the original class and 10 of the converted Class

625.3s were modified with Franco-Crosti boilers but this modification was not successful. The last of the Class 625s were withdrawn from regular service in 1976 although a number were retained as part of FS's strategic reserve of steam locomotives until 1998. In this view, No 625.157 is seen approaching Domodossola with a special on 1 June 1972. More than 20 of the type – but not No 625.157 – survive in preservation.
Les Folkard/Online Transport Archive

Above: On 1 June 1972 Class 640.088 is seen arriving at Chivasso with a short passenger train. Following the creation of FS in 1905, Giuseppe Zara, the Chief Mechanical Engineer, produced a number of standard designs for the railway. These included the Class 630 2-6-0; in 1907 it was decided to construct a superheated version of this type and the Class 640 was the result. The first 48 were constructed by Berliner Maschinenbau AG with the remainder being built in Italy by Società Italiana Ernesto Breda (103 locomotives), Costruzioni Meccaniche di Saronno (18) and Gio. Ansaldo & Co (four). Production ceased in 1911 by which stage 173 had been completed; this included four built for the Società Strade Ferrate di Biella (SFB; Biella Railway) which only passed to FS ownership on 10 July 1951 with the end of the SFB concession. A further 15 locomotives from Class 630 were equipped with superheaters between 1929 and 1931; these were designated as Class 640.3. The Class 640 was designed primarily for express passenger services but they were replaced by the more powerful Class 640 2-6-0 and Class 685 2-6-2 and relegated to secondary passenger duties. As such a number were to survive through until the late 1970s. Almost 20 – including No 640.088 – survive in preservation.
Les Folkard/Online Transport Archive

Above: With 370 being constructed between 1906 and 1922, the Class 835 0-6-0T represented FS's standard shunting locomotive. Based on the earlier Classes 825 and 830, the '835' used the larger boiler from the latter with the use of enlarged cylinders. After World War 2, three of the type ended up in Yugoslavia and were operated thereafter by JŽ. During the 1950s, the frames, wheels and coupling rods of 89 of the type were used in the construction of two types of electric shunter – the Classes E.321 (40 locomotives) and E.322 (20 locomotives) – as well as the Class D.234 diesel-hydraulic shunter. Some 30 Class 835 were still operational into the early 1980s and the final years of FS steam operation; the last were withdrawn in 1984. On 2 June 1972 No 835.231 is seen awaiting its next duty at Torino Smistamento. Due to the large number of locomotives retained as static exhibits on plinths near railway stations more than 50 of the class are still extant.
Les Folkard/Online Transport Archive

Right: Between 1912 and 1916 FS acquired 117 Class 875 2-6-0Ts for use on branch line traffic; simultaneously a second class of 2-6-0T was being constructed. This was the Class 880, which differed from Class 875 by being superheated. A total of 60 of Class 880 were constructed from new, whilst an additional 28 were converted from Class 875. By the early 1970s – when this view of No 880.047 was taken at Cuneo on the 5.6am service from Arrasca on 3 June 1972, the surviving members of the class – some 30 in all – were all based in northern Italy. The last of the unsuperheated Class 875 was withdrawn from Udine, where it had been station pilot, in 1971.
Les Folkard/Online Transport Archive

Below: The MÁV Class 601 2-6-6-0 four-cylinder Mallet-type locomotive, of which 60 were constructed by Magyar Királyi Államvasutak Gépgyára (MÁVAG; Hungarian Royal State Railways' Machine Factory) between 1914 and 1921, were the largest and most powerful steam locomotives constructed before World War 1. Designed primarily for freight traffic on heavily graded routes, a number of the class were based in Croatia and thus passed to Jugoslavenske Željeznice (JŽ; Yugoslavian State Railways – Jugoslavenske Državni Željeznice [JDŽ] until the 1950s) following World War 1. Numbered 32.001-36 by JŽ, one of the class – No 32.015 – is seen at Fiume (now known as Rijeka) in the late spring of 1959. The class was used on freight traffic from the port to the city of Karlstadt (now Karlovac) some 81 miles inland on the main line to Zagreb. *Online Transport Archive*

Opposite above: On 13 May 1964 JŽ 760mm gauge Class 85 2-8-2 No 85.022 departs from Obrenovac, in the western suburbs of Belgrade, with a passenger service. The Class 85 was first introduced in 1930 with 35 being constructed; these were originally numbered 1501-35. A further 20 – Nos 85.036-45 – were constructed by Đuro Đaković of Slavonski Brod later. The locomotives were the standard heavy duty mixed traffic locomotive used on the narrow-gauge line connecting Belgrade with the Bosnian 760mm network at Sarajevo, which was completed in the 1920s. The Bosnian section of the line closed in 1974 and the last section in Serbia closed in 1983. *Charles Firminger/Bob Bridger Collection/Online Transport Archive*

Above: Sremska Mitrovica is the administrative centre of the Srem District, to the west of Belgrade and to the south of the River Danube. On 14 May 1964 Class 38 No 38.008 is seen approaching Sremska Mitrovica station from the east with a passenger service. In 1946 the Vulcan Foundry of Newton-le-Willows in England constructed 120 'Liberation' class 2-8-0s for use on heavy freight trains in post-war Europe. Based upon the earlier wartime 'Austerity' 2-8-0, designed by Robert A. Riddles, 65 of the type were acquired by JŽ, with the remainder being sent to Czechoslovakia (Class 459.0), Luxembourg (Class 47) and Poland (Class Tr202). A further 10 were constructed by Đuro Đaković during 1957 and 1958. One of the Yugoslav-built examples – No 38.072 – survives as do two of the 30 Polish examples.
Charles Firminger/Bob Bridger Collection/Online Transport Archive

Above: Brosanski Brod – known since 2009 simply as Brod – is in the extreme north of Bosnia and is part of the Serbian part of the country. On 16 May 1964 Class 73 2-6-2 No 73.001 is seen departing from the station with the 2.5pm service to Usora. The locomotive is one of a class of 23 built to the design of Krauss & Co of Linz and new in 1907; 15 were built by Krauss with the remaining eight being constructed by Magyar Királyi Államvasutak Gépgyára (MÁVAG) of Budapest. The class was originally designated IIIb5 and was designed for light passenger duties.

Three of the class – No 73.002 plus two of the MÁVAG-built examples (Nos 73.018/19) – survive in preservation. Brosanski Brod was the northernmost terminus of the 760mm gauge line which opened from Žepče on 22 April 1879 courtesy of the Imperial and Royal Bosnian Railway which became part of the Bosnia-Herzegovina State Railway in 1895. The line from Brosanski Brod to Dervanta closed on 26 May 1969.
Charles Firminger/Bob Bridger Collection/Online Transport Archive

Right: Following work to upgrade sections of main line in the late 1920s to permit higher axle loading, JDŽ acquired 110 new standard steam locomotives from 1930: 40 4-6-2s, 30 2-8-2s and 40 2-10-0s. The 2-8-2s were originally designated Class 486 (Nos 486.301-30) but were subsequently renumbered 06.001-30. All 30 were built by Borsig and, in their later career, were to be found concentrated in the area to the west of Zagreb. Here No 06.005 is pictured shunting at Celje in Slovenia. *Bernard Harrison/Bob Bridger Collection/Online Transport Archive*

Above: After World War 1 it was decided to construct a batch of 4-8-0 locomotives for use on the Western Railway in Austria as a consequence of increasing train loads caused by the replacement of old wooden-built coaches by more modern steel-bodied examples. A total of 40 of BBÖ Class 113 were constructed between 1923 and 1928 by StEG. Following the Anschluss in 1938, Deutsche Reichsbahn reclassified them as Class 33. Five of the type – Nos 10.001-5 – ended up in the ownership of JŽ after the war and here, on 5 July 1966, the first of the quintet is seen outside the shed at Ljubljana. Sister locomotive No 10.005 is preserved but in the guise of BBÖ No 113.32.
Bernard Harrison/Bob Bridger Collection/Online Transport Archive

Right: The creation of the state of Yugoslavia included the former Hungarian province of Croatia and, as a result, a number of MÁV designs were operated by JŽ. Although a significant number of these had been withdrawn and scrapped before 1933, many others were to survive into the post-World War 2 era. Amongst the 0-6-0s inherited by JŽ was the 43-strong Class 126. These had originally been MÁV Class 325, of which 247 were built between 1893 and 1907. Apart from MÁV and JŽ a number of the type were also operated by CFR and ČSD. Here, on 6 July 1966, No 126.043 is pictured in light steam at Zagreb awaiting its next duty.
Les Folkard/Online Transport Archive

Left: In order to exploit the rich forests that cover much of countries such as Yugoslavia and Romania, networks of narrow gauge railways were constructed. One such example was the 760mm Bosnische Forstindustrie AG promoted by Otto Steinbeis that developed into the Steinbeis Railway in Bosnia-Herzegovina that eventually extended over some 245 route miles in the area south of Prijedor. Passing through various hands, the railway survived World War 2 – albeit suffering severe damage – before becoming part of JŽ after the war. The line received a number of additional locomotives after the war, courtesy of the United Nations Relief and Rehabilitation Administration (UNRRA), but the construction of a competing standard gauge line from Novi Grad to Knin via Bihać undermined the line's economics. The narrow gauge network was progressively closed between 1969 and 1978. From opening in 1902, the line used a number of 0-4-4-0T Mallet locomotives including No 3 – seen here with a timber train near Lisina on 8 July 1966 – which was supplied by Maffei in 1902.
Les Folkard/Online Transport Archive

Above: Two of the Steinbeis Railway's UNRRA 0-8-0s – Nos 34 and 6 – are seen heading a service from Prijedor to Srnetica on 8 July 1966. The design of the locomotives was undertaken by the Pittsburgh-based H. K. Porter Co in 1941 and were delivered to the railway during 1945 and 1946 in order to assist in the reopening of the line following the damages and losses caused by World War 2. The locomotives, despite their relatively light axle loading, proved to be successful on the winding narrow gauge lines. Unusually, the locomotives were not renumbered into the JŽ and retained their UNRRA numbers throughout their operational career. A number of the type are still extant in the former Yugoslavia.
Les Folkard/Online Transport Archive

Above: In the late 19th century, the land that formed the future Yugoslavia was within the Austro-Hungarian empire and the development of much of the country's railway system was a consequence of that. As a result of the sizeable 760mm situated to the north, a number of narrow gauge lines were constructed serving Bosnia and Herzegovina. These included the Spalato Railway that connected the Steinbeis Railway to the Bosnia Railway. The first section from Lašva to Travnik opened in 1893 being extended thence via Donji Vakuf to Bugojno – including a 14-mile rack section – in 1894 with a line from Donji Vakuf to Jajce in 1895. On 9 July 1966 0-6-0T No 97.004 is seen at the junction station at Donji Vakuf with the 7.7am service from Jajce to Lašva. All of the narrow gauge railways serving Bosnia had closed by the end of 1979.
Bernard Harrison/Bob Bridger Collection/Online Transport Archive

Above: The first of the ex-DR Class 52 'Kriegslok' 2-10-0s appeared in Yugoslavia during World War 2 but, after the war, JŽ received 341 examples as war reparations. This made the type the single largest class of steam locomotive to operate in Yugoslavia; they were also the last steam locomotives to enter service with JŽ. The type saw service on both passenger and freight duties although, with electrification of certain lines, their area of operation became more restricted. Despite this a number remained operational in Croatia until the early 1980s and a handful were still in industrial use in Bosnia in 2017. After withdrawal, a significant number were held as part of the JŽ strategic reserve until the dissolution of Yugoslavia fallowing the death of Tito. Here, on 9 July 1966, oil-fired No 33.252 is seen passing through Lasva with a freight service heading towards Sarajevo.
Bernard Harrison/Bob Bridger Collection/Online Transport Archive

Above: Between 1942 and 1944 the US Army Transportation Corps took delivery of 382 0-6-0Ts designed by Howard G. Hill. Designated Class S100, the locomotives were designed for use in Europe after D-Day. With the cessation of hostilities in 1945, the locomotives were sold to a number of European railway companies and JŽ acquired 106; the locomotives were to become Class 62 in Yugoslavia. Further locomotives were built by Đuro Đaković of Croatia between 1952 and 1961. One of the US-built examples – No 62.100 – is seen here on 9 July 1966 being coupled to a passenger service at Sisak. A number of US-built Class 62s – but not No 62.100 – survive in preservation.
Les Folkard/Online Transport Archive